MAMETZ

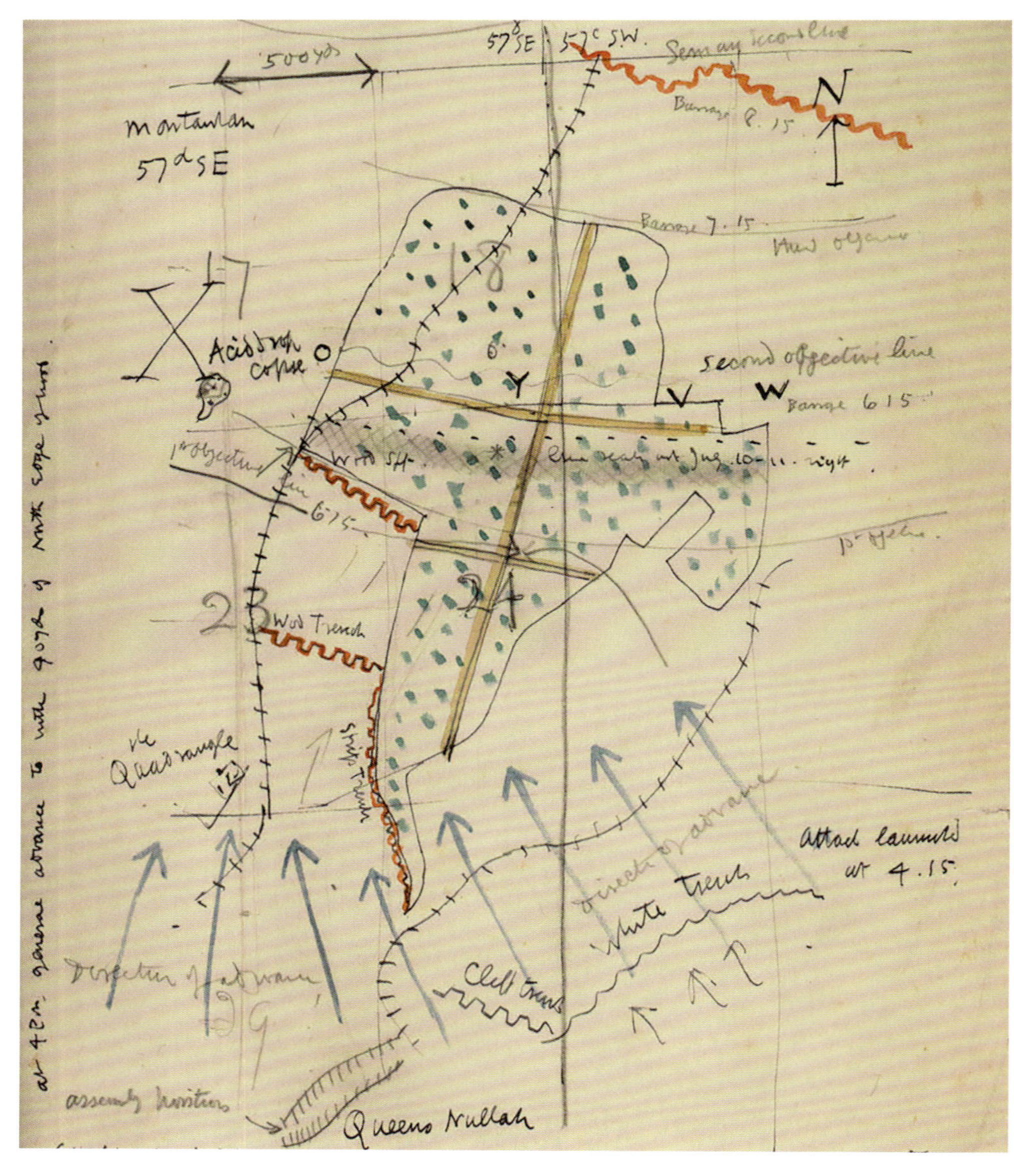

500 yds
Montauban 57d SE
57d SE
57c SW.
Seems any Iccons line
Barrage 8.15.
N
Barrage 7.15.
New Organs
Acid Drop Copse O
second objective line
Barrage 6.15"
Y
V
W
1st Objective line
Wood SH.
Line seary out Aug. 10-11. night
6.15"
p". of line.
2 3
Wood Trench
3 A
the Quadrangle
Strip Trench
Direction of advance
White Trench
Attack launched at 4.15.
Cliff trench
Direction of advance
assembly positions
Queens Nullah

MAMETZ

Aled Rhys Hughes

Essay by Jeremy Hooker

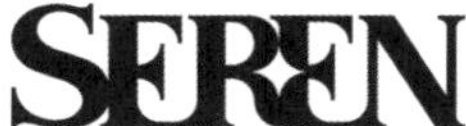

SEREN
is the book imprint of
Poetry Wales Press Ltd.
57 Nolton Street, Bridgend, Wales, CF31 3AE

www.serenbooks.com
facebook.com/SerenBooks
twitter: @SerenBooks

Photographs © Aled Rhys Hughes, 2016.

Essay © Jeremy Hooker, 2016
David Jones' map of Mametz Wood reproduced with the
permission of the National Library of Wales.

ISBN 978-1-78172-328-9

A CIP record for this title is available
from the British Library.

The publisher works with the financial
assistance of the Welsh Books Council.

Author website: www.aledrhyshughes.co.uk

Printed in the Czech Republic
by Akcent Media Ltd.

Contents

Foreword

After re-reading David Jones's long war poem *In Parenthesis* in the early summer of 2009, I consulted my French Atlas; I could make a short detour on a planned trip to Paris from the A1 Autoroute and visit Mametz. When I arrived the village was considerably smaller than I had imagined, and surprisingly at the cross-road there was a Welsh language road sign (38 Welsh Division Memorial). The road became narrower and forked: I took the right hand turn which became a farm track leading to a small car park. In it was parked a bus with 'Edwards South Wales' emblazoned across its flank; I was in the correct place.

I knew very little about the Somme or the First World War. However I had seen photographs; a landscape of limbless and leafless trees surrounded by craters and mud in what seemed like perpetual winter. It was only after researching that I discovered that the trees were leafless even in summer, as the blasts from the shells had defoliated them.

July 2009 was hot, searingly hot, the fields were full of golden wheat and barley, and the sky had perfect cotton-wool clouds against its warm blue. Just across these fields, towering high, were the trees of Mametz Wood. It was difficult to find a way in, but once through a gap it was as though night had instantly descended. I felt this duality. The cultivated fields gave way to tangled trees, branches and briars, and also, unmistakably, craters. How could they have survived for almost a hundred years?

As a photographer I wanted to make images immediately, it was far too dark to attempt anything without the tripod, so in gathering my equipment the process of thinking about what to photograph was under way. I have an interest in named places, and have photographed such locations so that I could use the title with the image. One of the place names from *In Parenthesis* that had stuck was, 'The Hammerhead'. Two photographs came immediately; both images seemed to deal with expanse vs confinement and light vs dark.

Acid Drop Copse, the Quadrangle, Queens Nullah, Happy Valley and Death Valley are such image-laden names. Photographing these named places would be my way of establishing the ground, much like the soldiers had during the war, since naming something gives a hold or handle on it.

That first visit proved to be the beginning of a long-term project that saw me return to Mametz Wood, on as close a date to the 10th of July as possible, for the next six years – the 38th Welsh division captured the Wood from the German army on the 10th July 1916. I wanted the photographs to have a visual consistency.

Each July was different. Some years the fields held potatoes, 8-foot sweet corn on two occasions, and wheat or barley on other visits. In the last three years a lot of trees from the Hammerhead section had been felled; counting the rings on the stumps confirmed that all were in their nineties. I arranged for a botanist to accompany me on one visit to see if she could identify trees that survived World War I. In a small fraction of the wood's 200 acres she identified a few candidates, but could not be sure. Our discussion, however, led me to look at the trees with marks and scars and photograph these witness bearers.

Walking around and through Mametz Wood extraordinary things appear. Unexploded shells lifted from the ground by growing trees, shoes and lamps from dugouts, German belt buckles and Mills Mk4 grenades lying unceremoniously among the foliage. It is also obvious from the presence of modern plastic shotgun cartridges that the wood is still used as a hunting ground, and pheasants scatter into the undergrowth and deer leap quickly away as you approach.

I did not meet a single person in the wood, but presences

linger of soldiers long ago, and of more recent visitors with their mementos. Small wooden crosses are pinned to some trees and photographs and names of Welsh soldiers carefully placed on others. Perhaps most poignant were the Welsh flags, nailed at their corners into the trees. Most flags have been there for so long that they seem subsumed by their hosts.

Over the years I have researched and learned more about David Jones and why he wrote *In Parenthesis*. Some of his words have affected my images, like the phrase "Keep date with the genius of the place…" (66). There is so much depth in *In Parenthesis* that it requires multiple readings and investigations; Mametz Wood affects me, exactly how is indefinable, but the need for many visits and image making is real.

On his map of the wood David Jones clearly identifies the first and second objectives for the 38th Division. Between them is the central ride, literally the place where the forest owners would ride their horses. Photographing from the second objective line towards the first down the ride produced an idyllic image of the wood; how different it would have been in 1916.

The most challenging images to make were the four images of twilight. The photographs are a direct response to three sentences from *In Parenthesis*:

> "Things seen precisely just now lost exactness. …[the] wood became only a darker shape uncertainly expressed. Your eyes begin to strain after escaping definitions." (98)

The soldiers in the trenches were most fearful at twilight, as it was the perfect time for an enemy attack. Photography is usually associated with clarity and precision, however the complete opposite was required in these four images if I was to attempt to escape their definitions.

People come, mostly by car, to visit the Dragon Gallois, and the signposts have become clearer over the last few years with the anticipation of thousands of visitors during the 2016 commemorations. Usually they clamber up the steps, take a photograph of the dragon and drive on to the next memorial; "Cook's tourists" as David Jones referred to them. (Thomas Cook organised battlefield tours as early as 1919). Some however stay for longer; many would be Welsh visitors, a family association perhaps?

The annual return to make images was my way of avoiding touristic pitfalls, and an attempt to get a 'clearer' view of what happened at Mametz Wood a century ago. But However long I stayed the fighting, and the reasons for it, remained beyond my reach, but I hope these images are a suitable commemoration of the men who took part and the land over which they fought.

– ALED RHYS HUGHES

CONFRONTATION

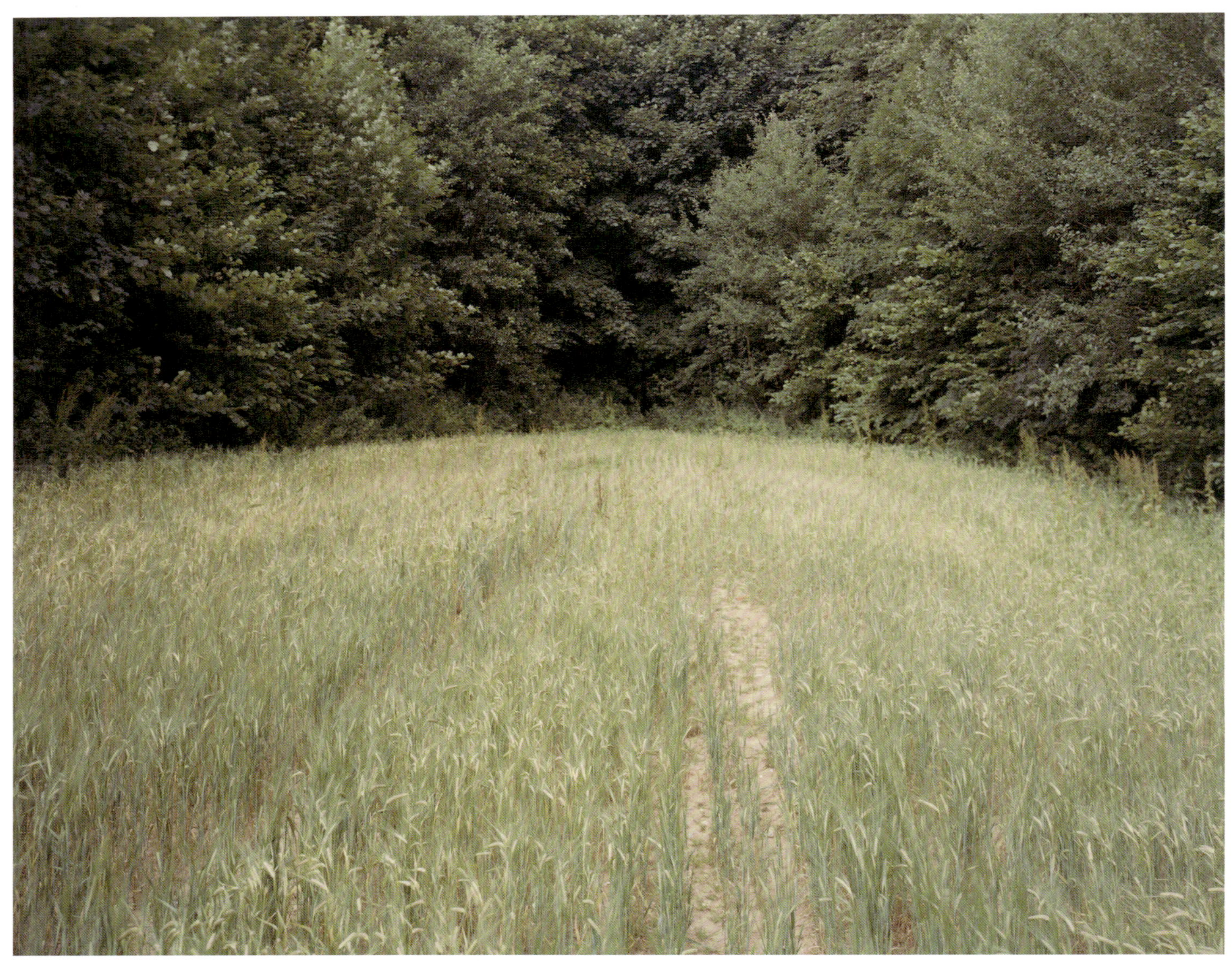

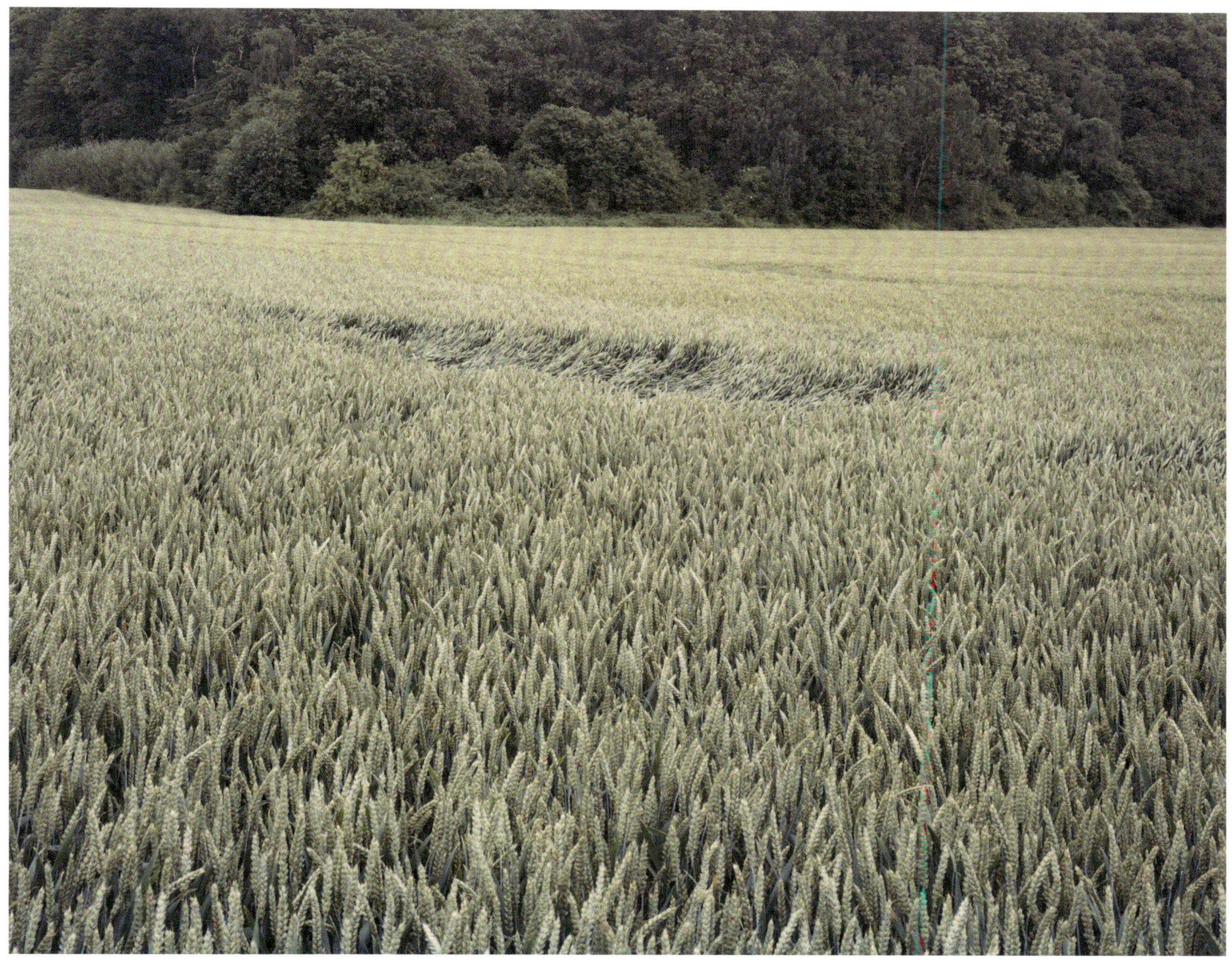

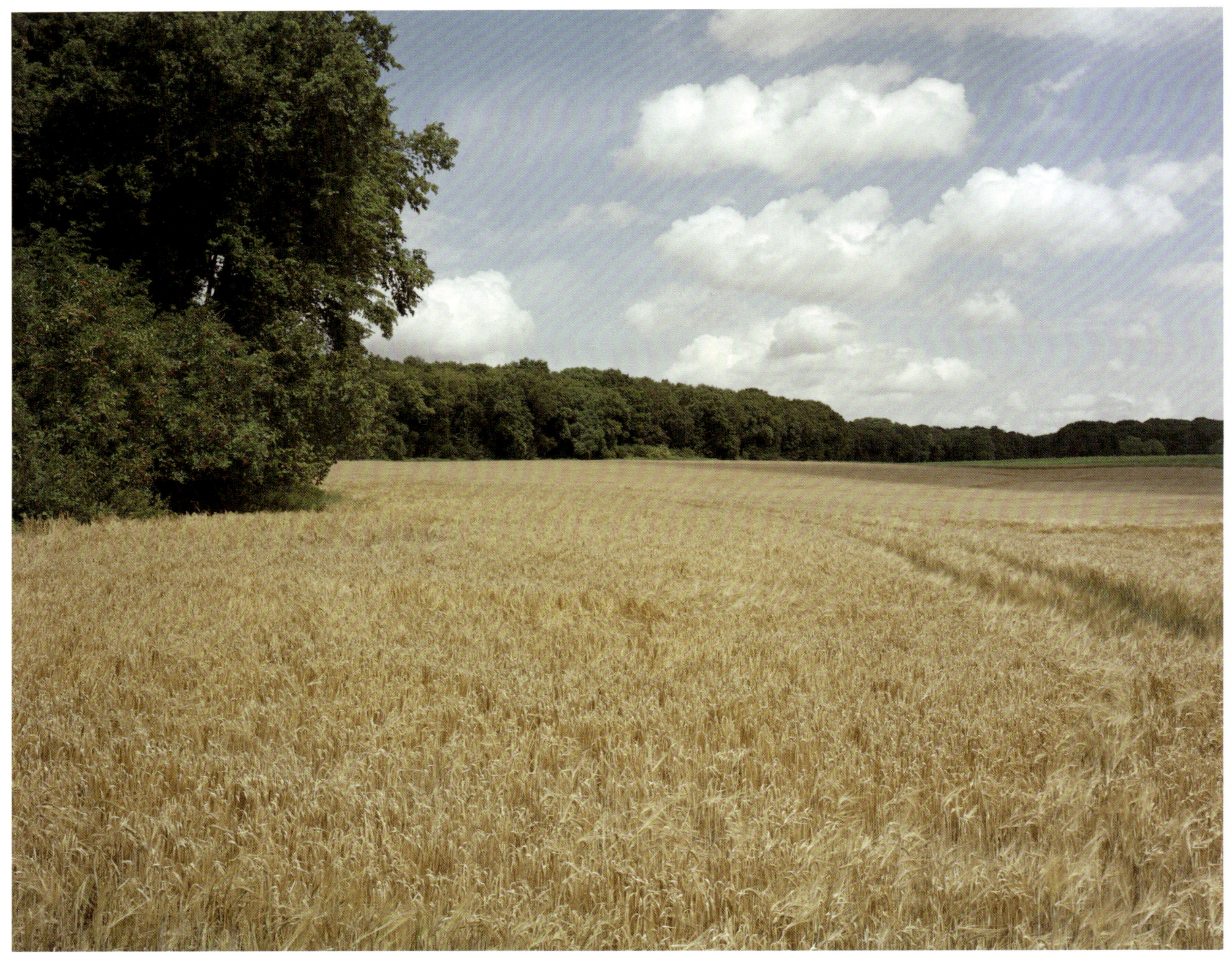

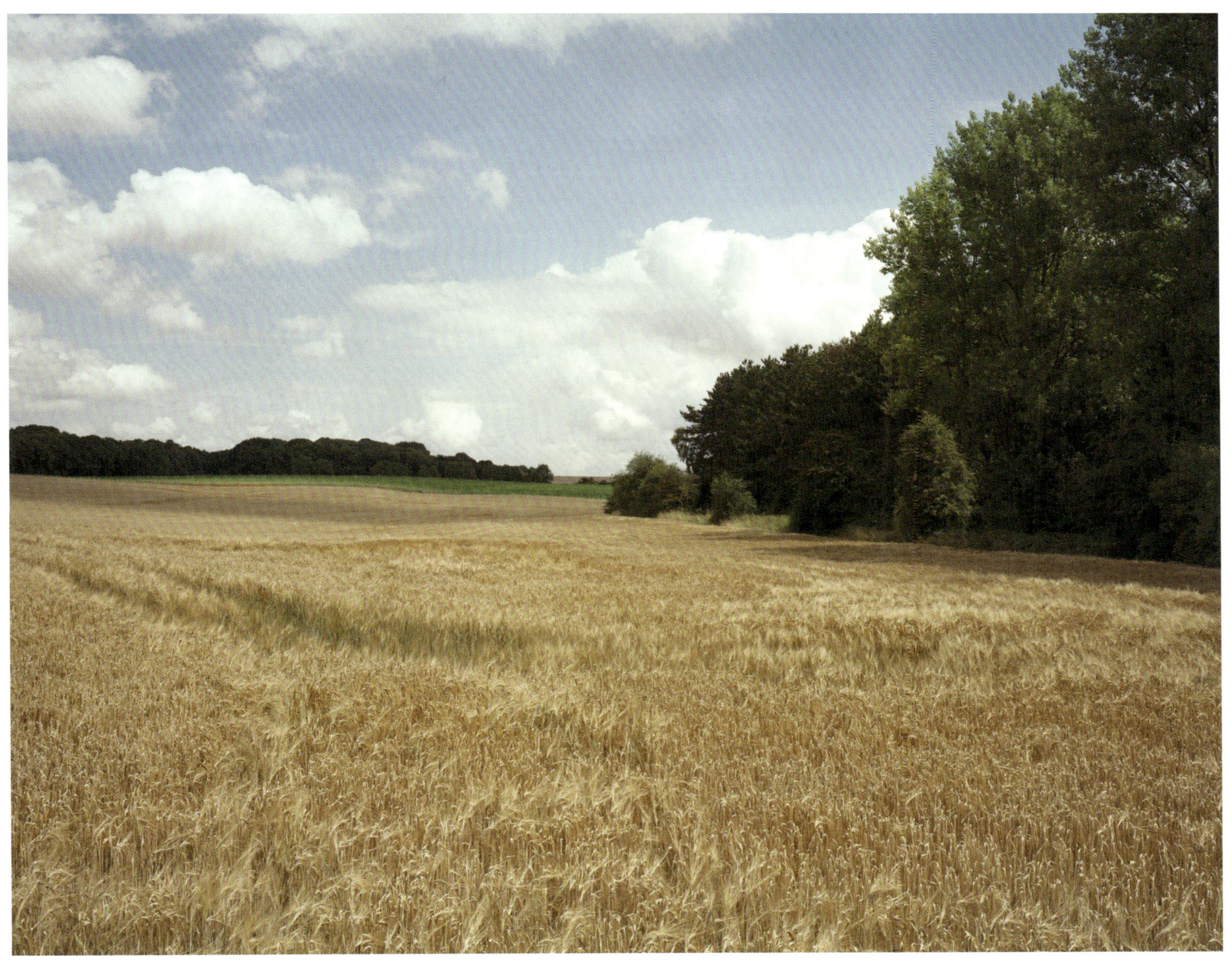

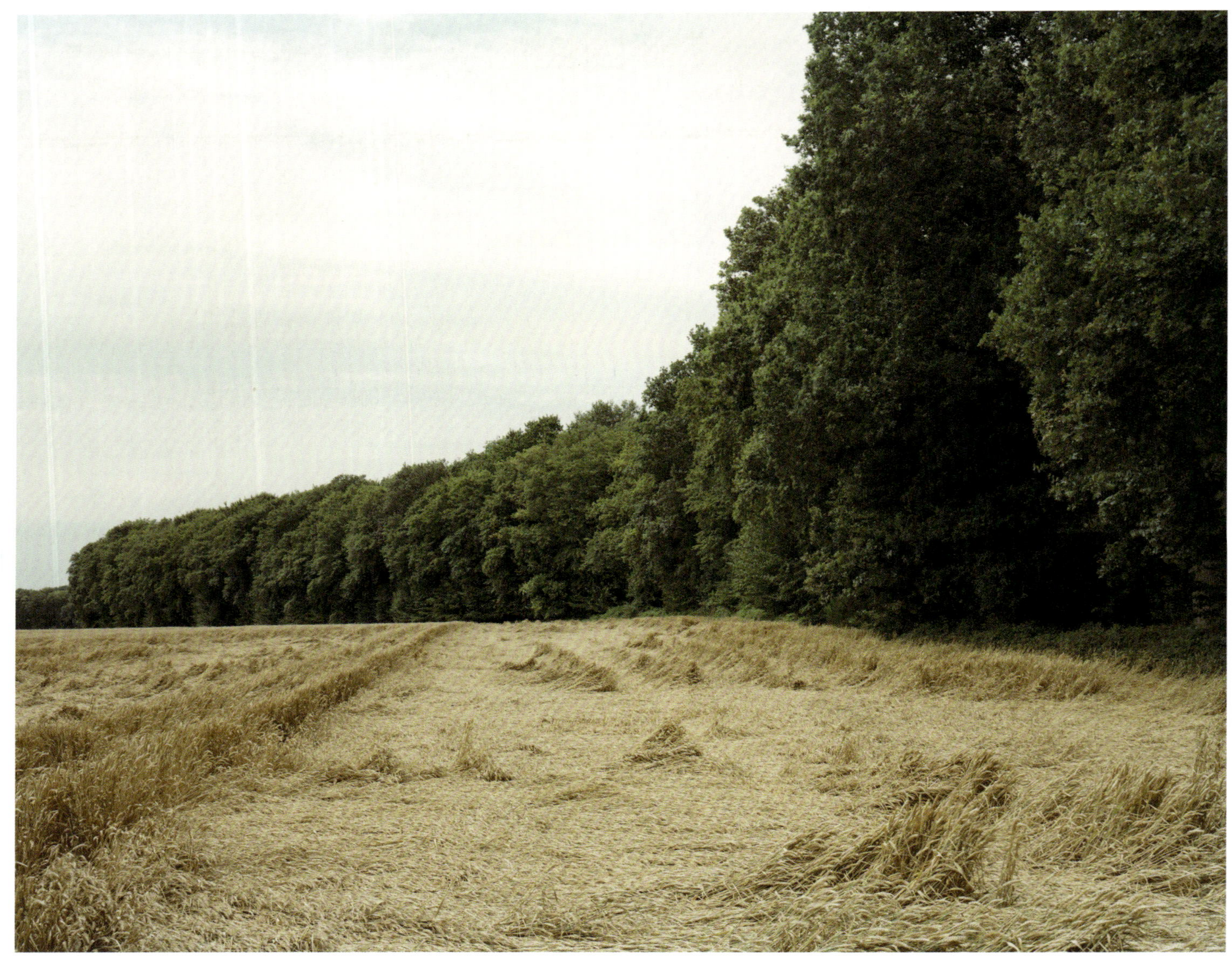

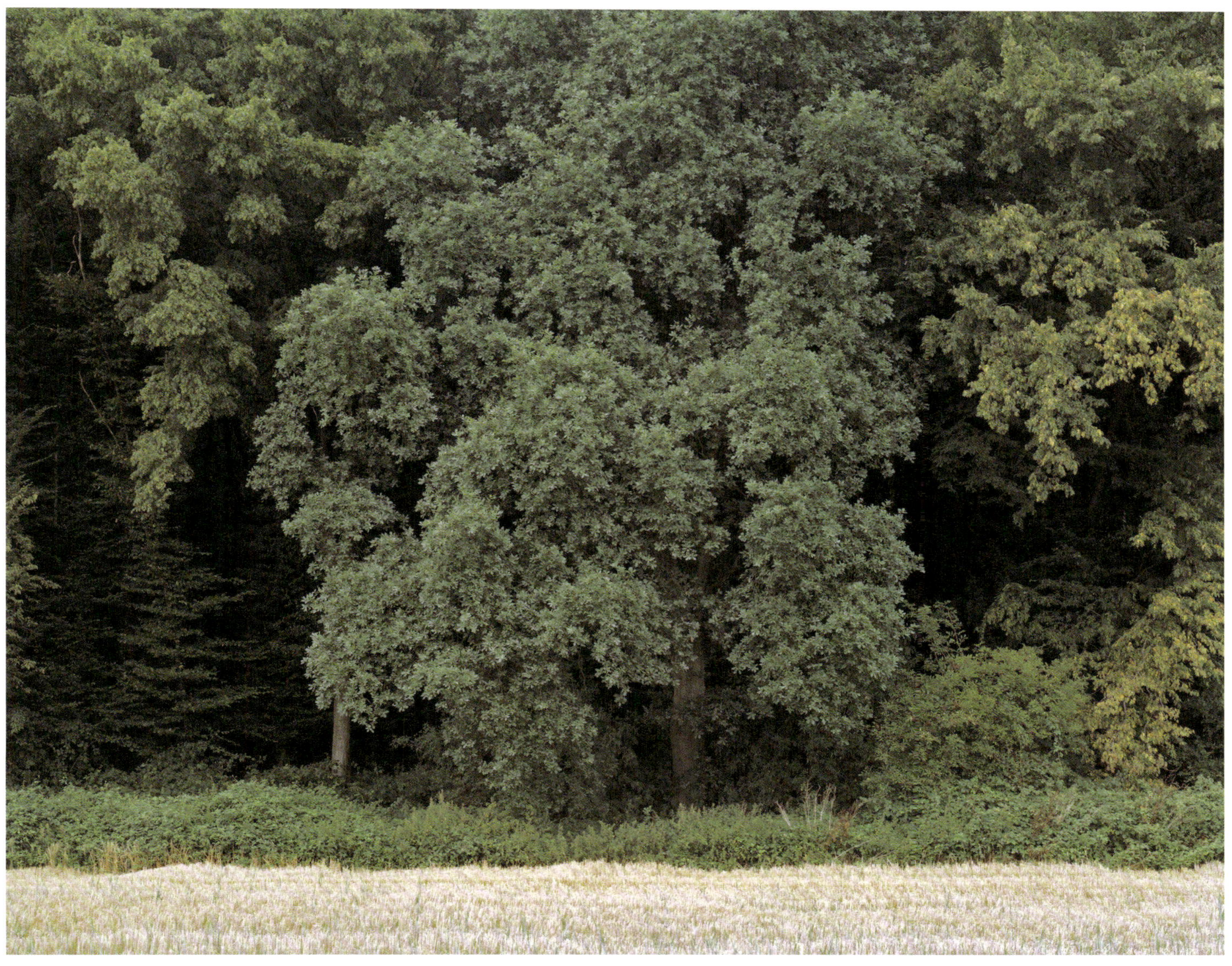

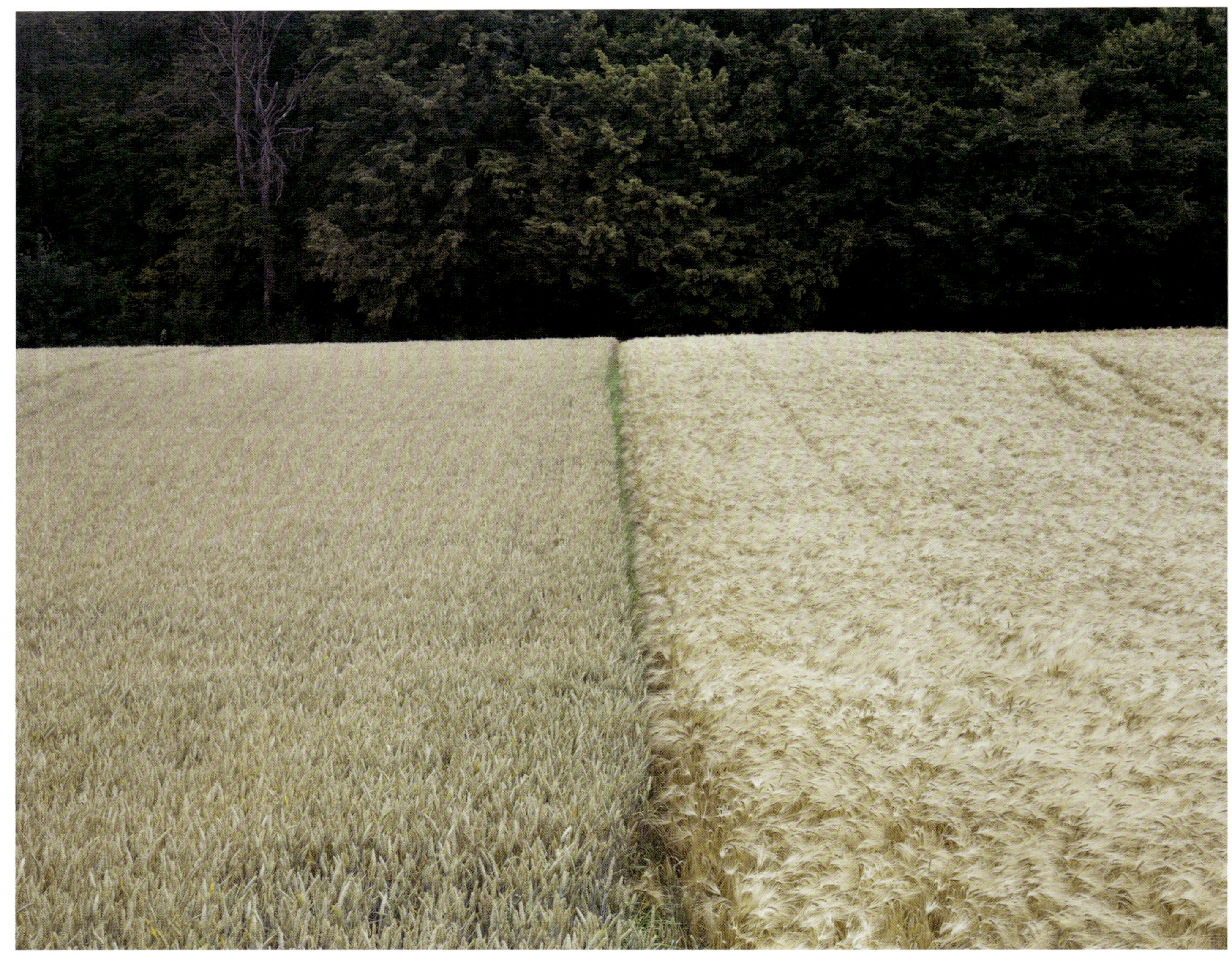

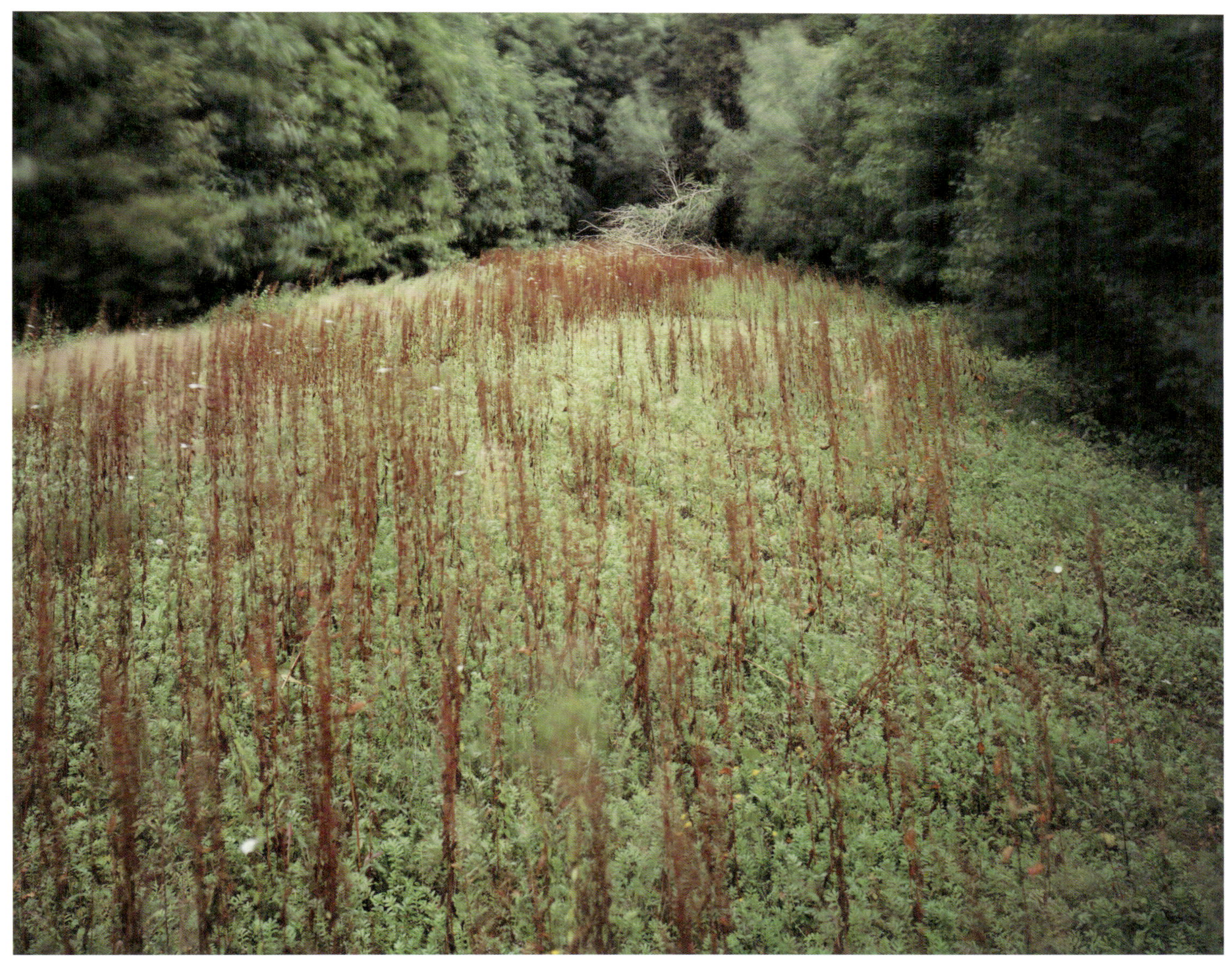

PLACES

White Trench
Queens Nullah
Traverse View
The Quadrangle
Acid Drop Copse

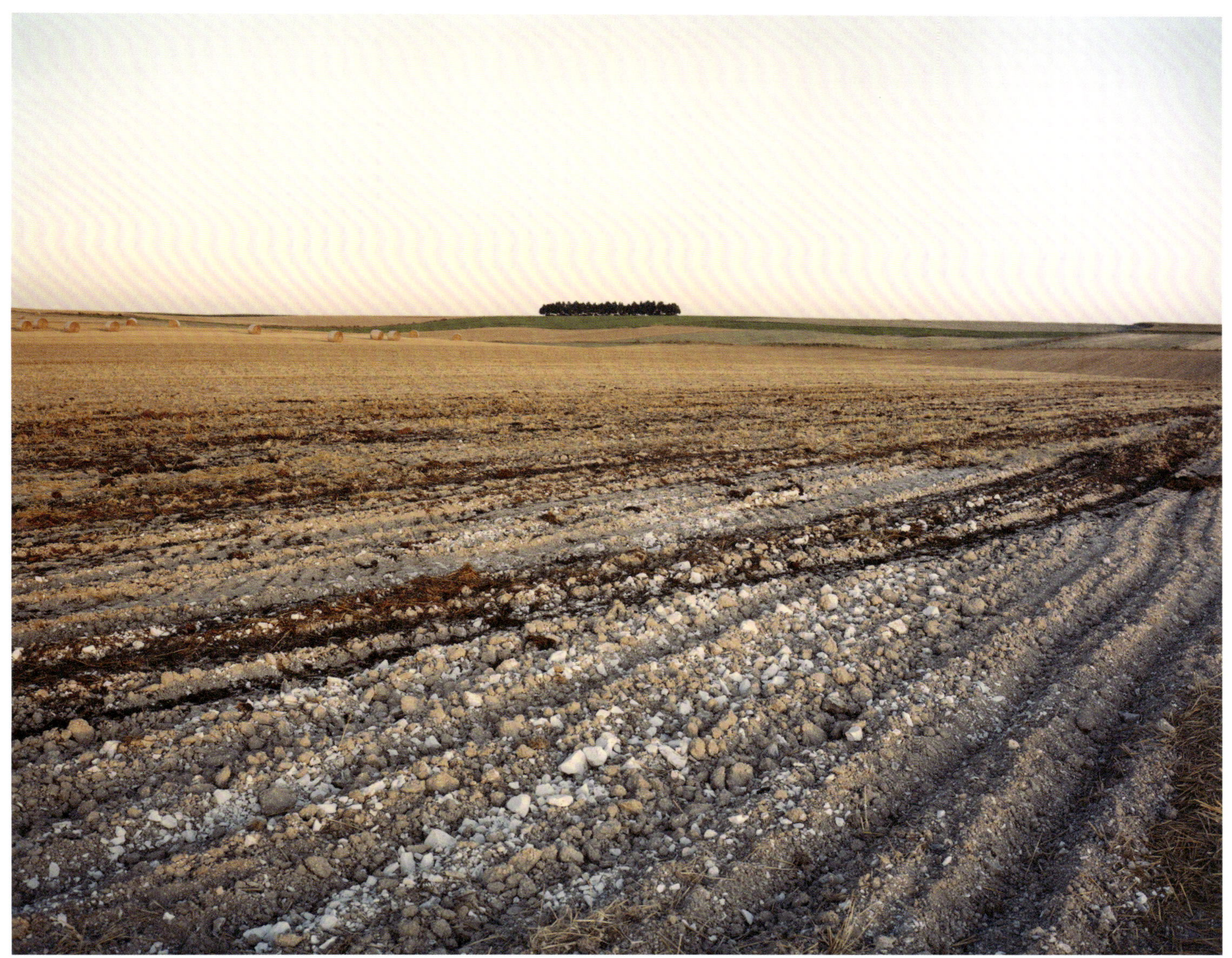

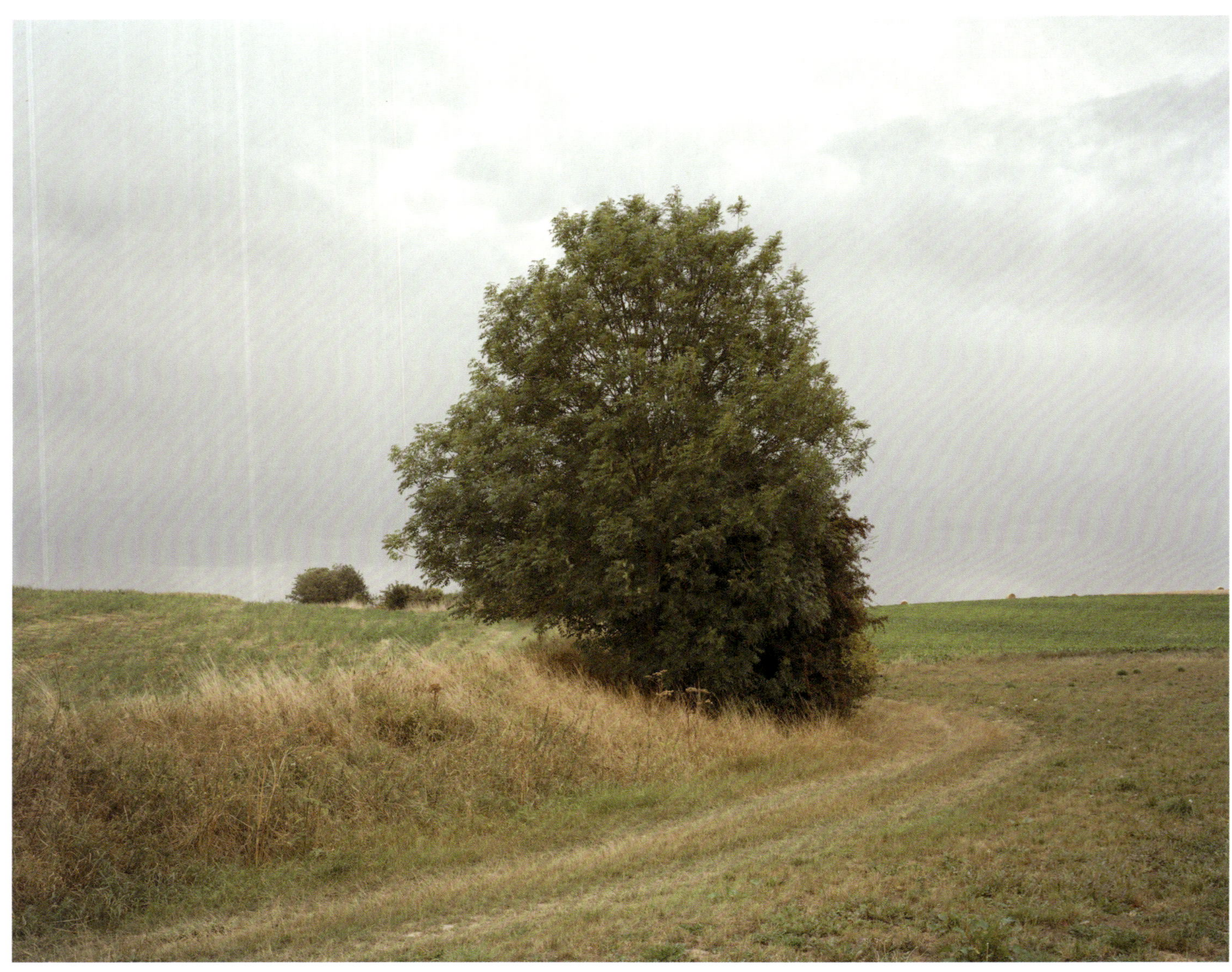

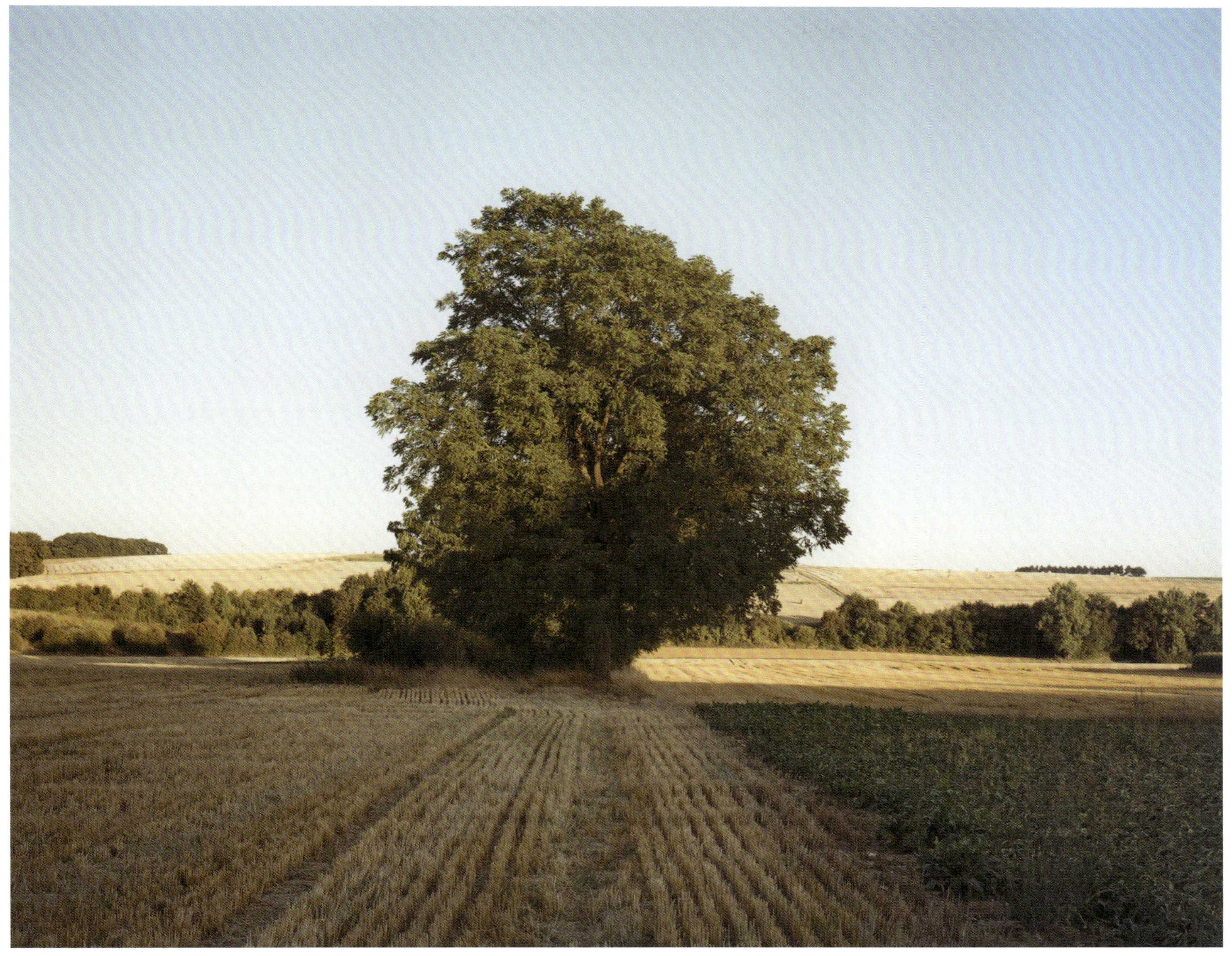

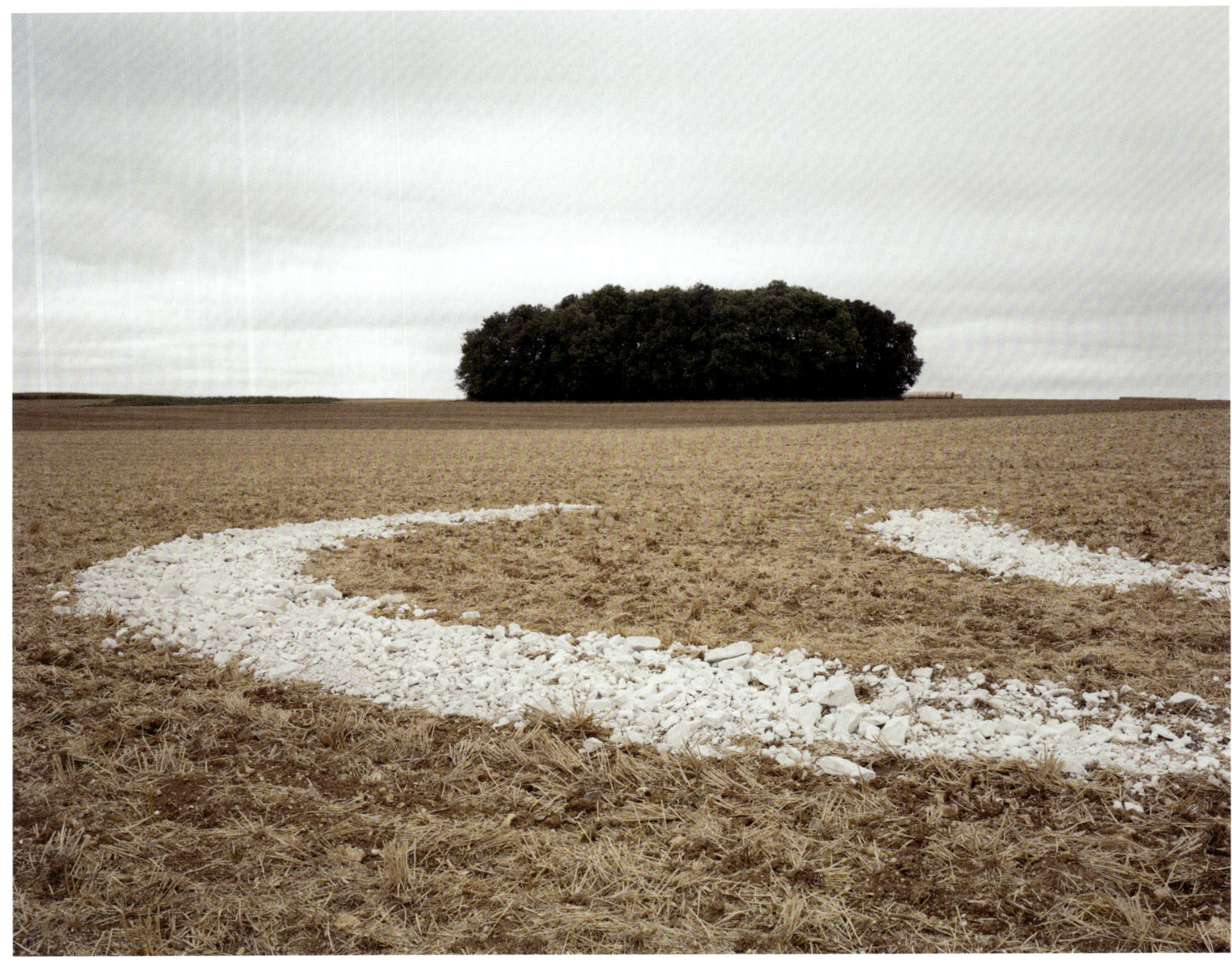

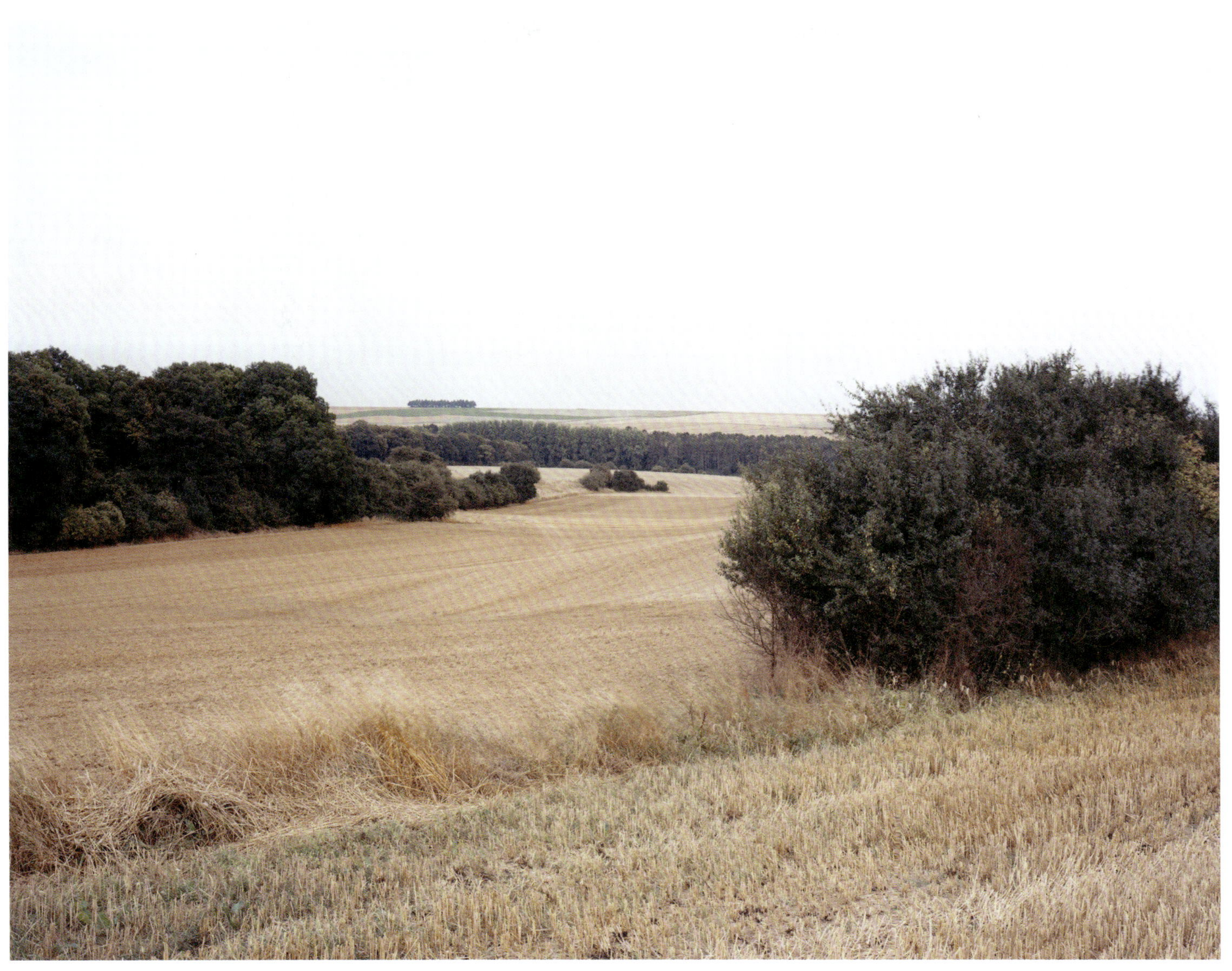

SHELLS

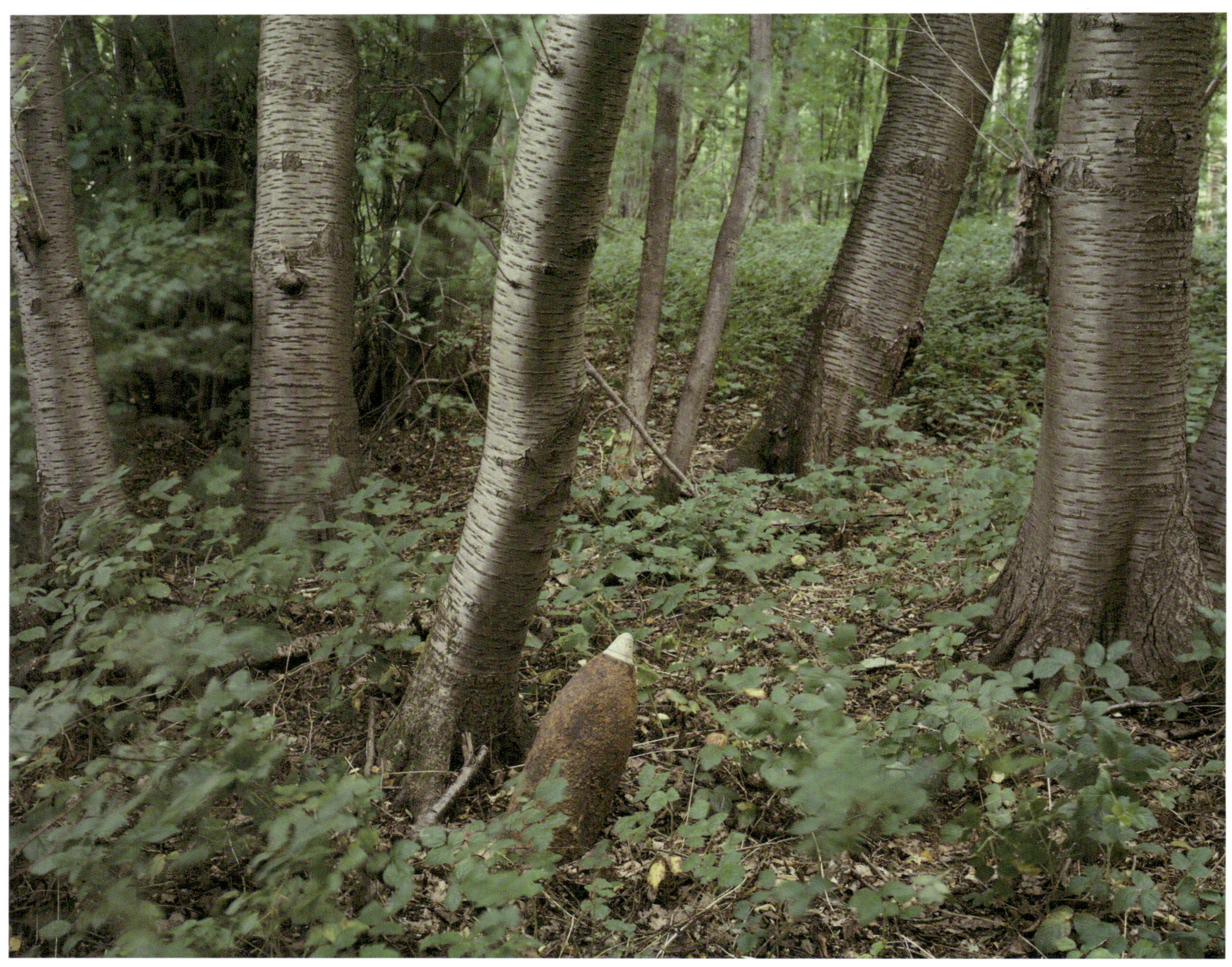

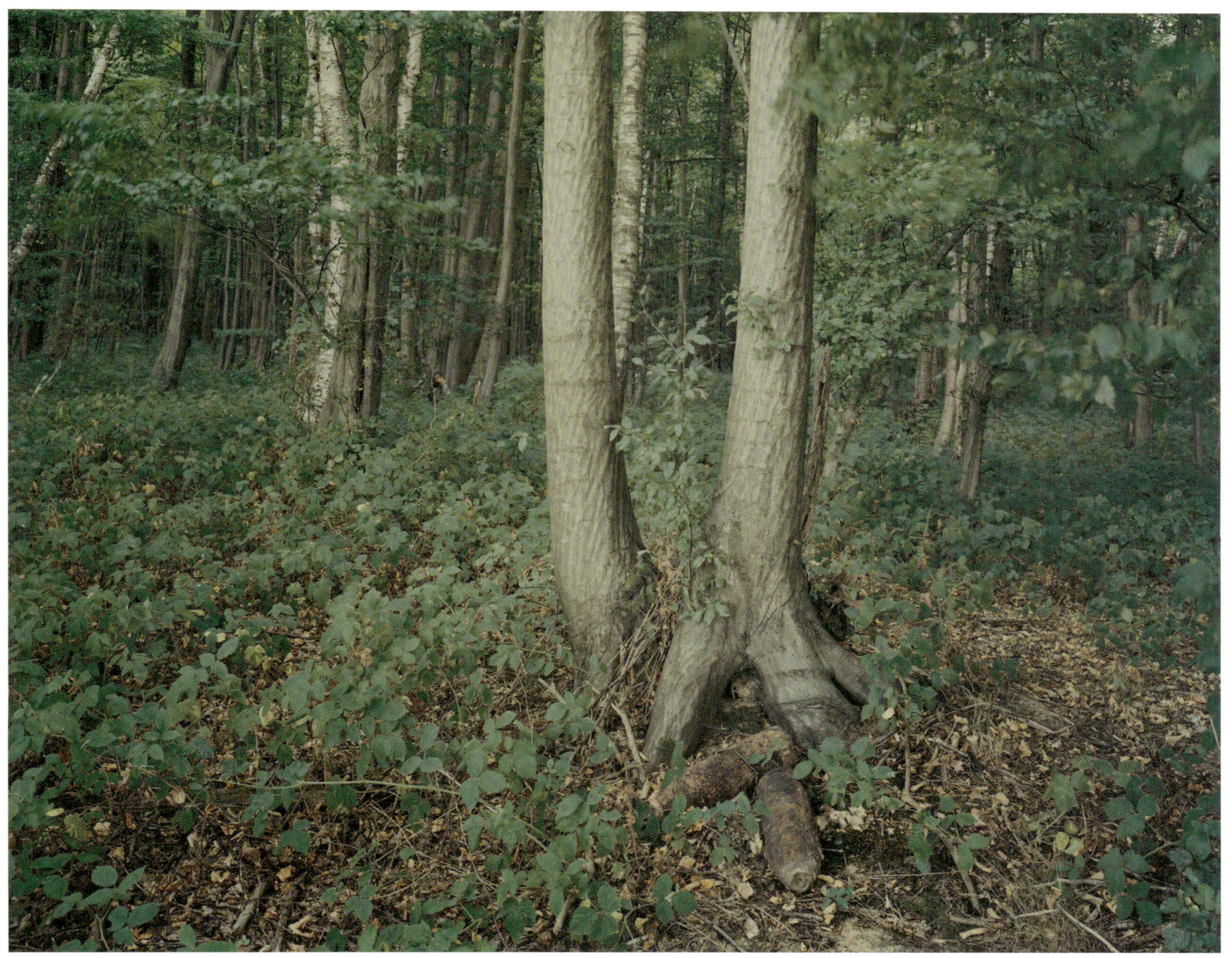

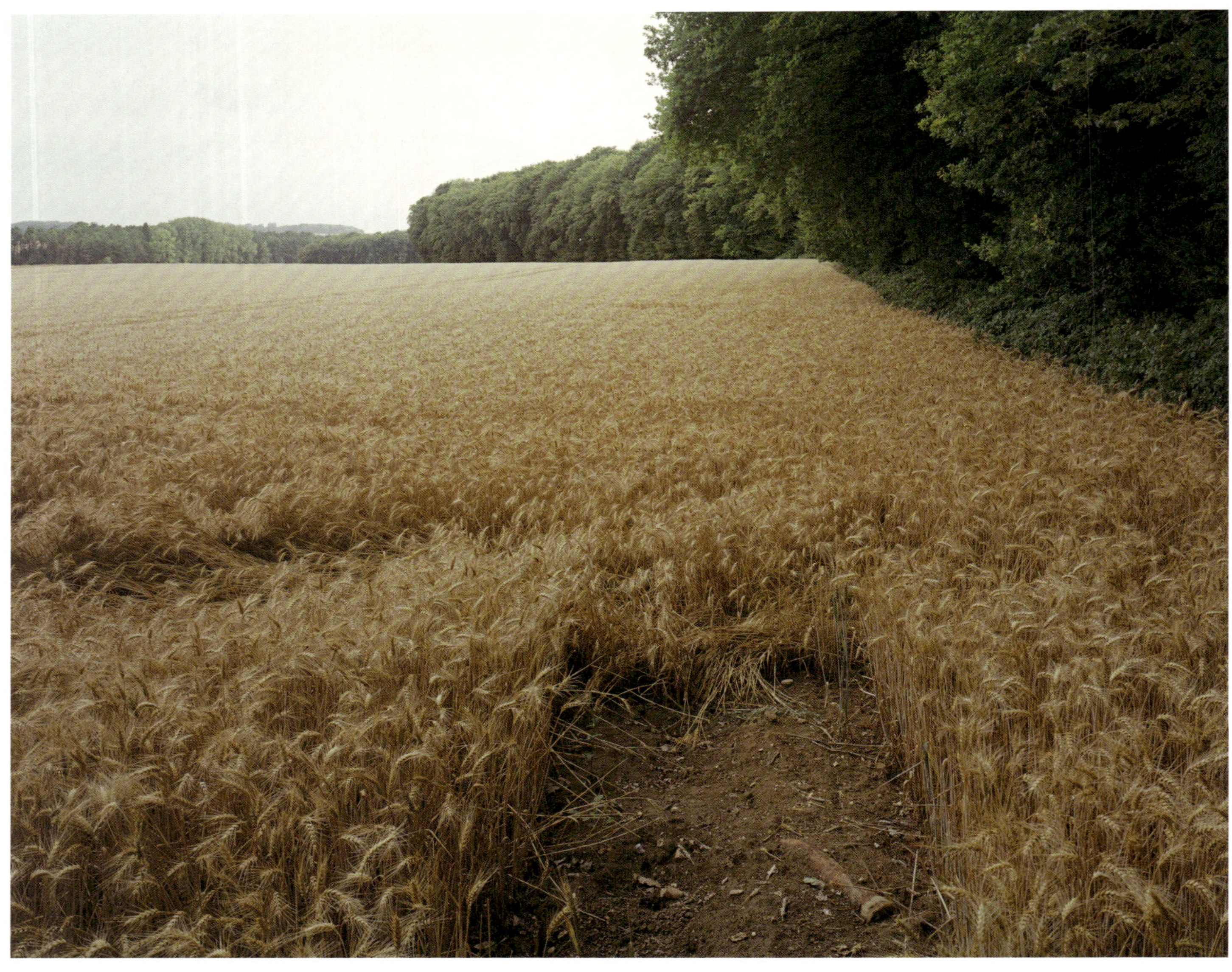

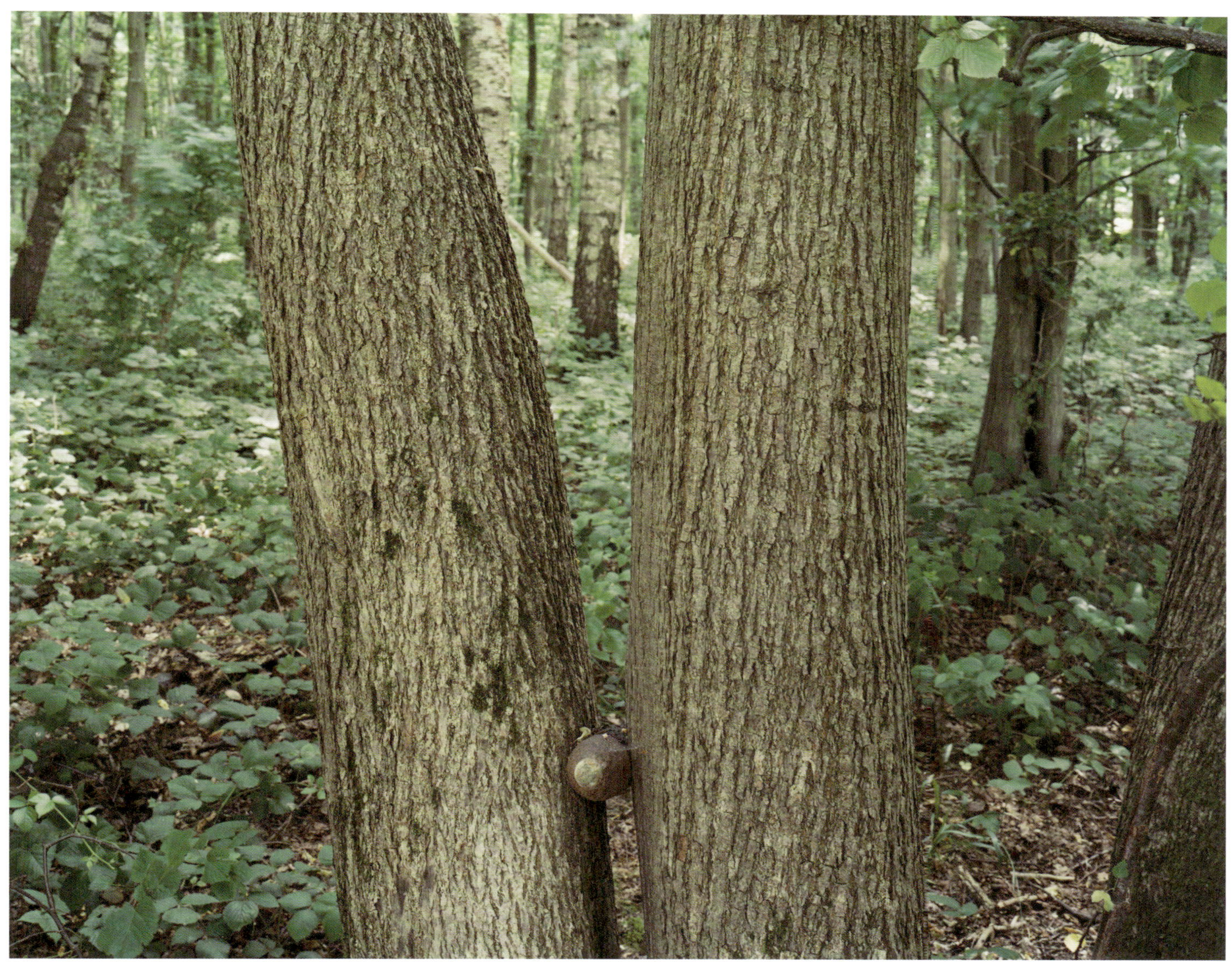

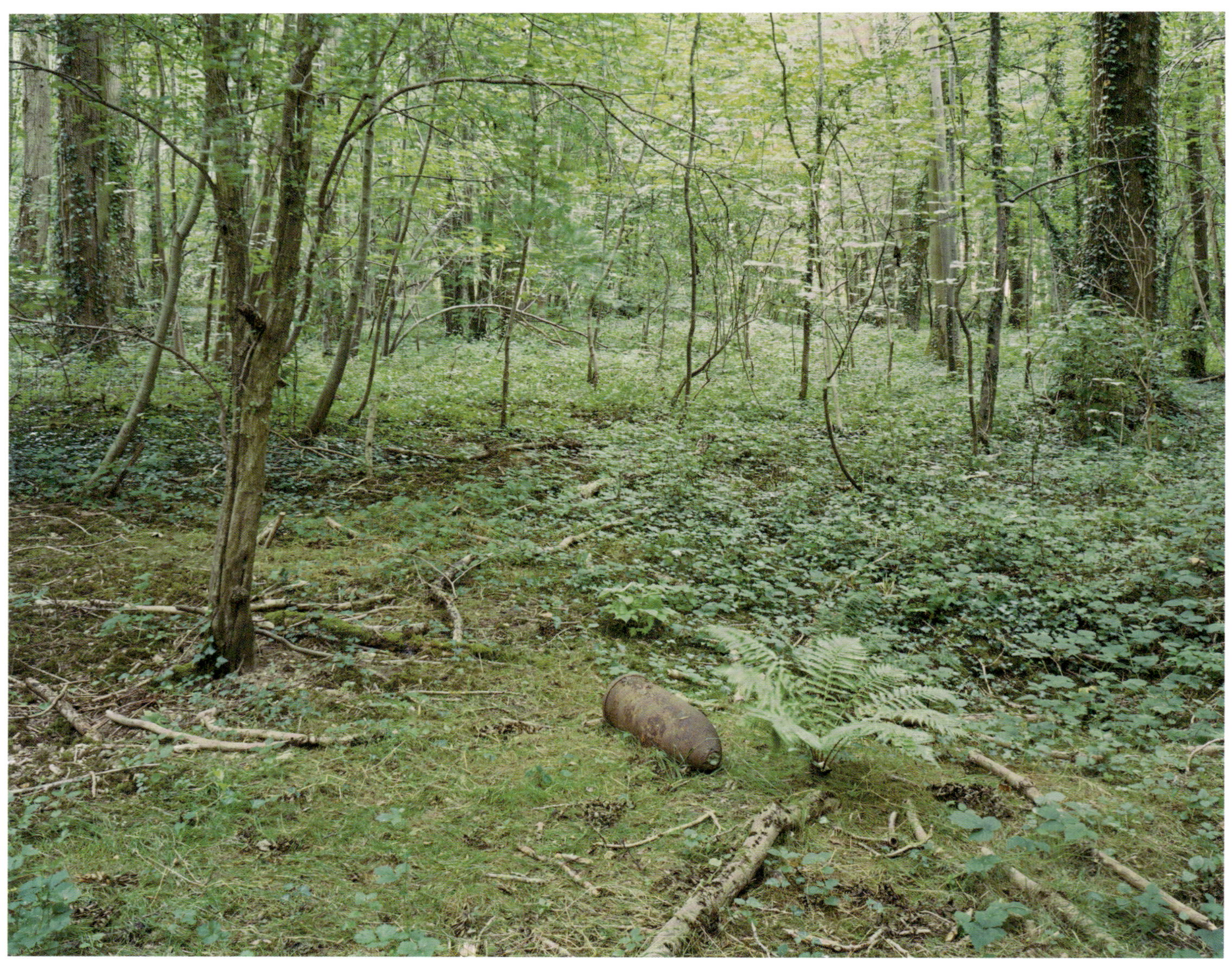

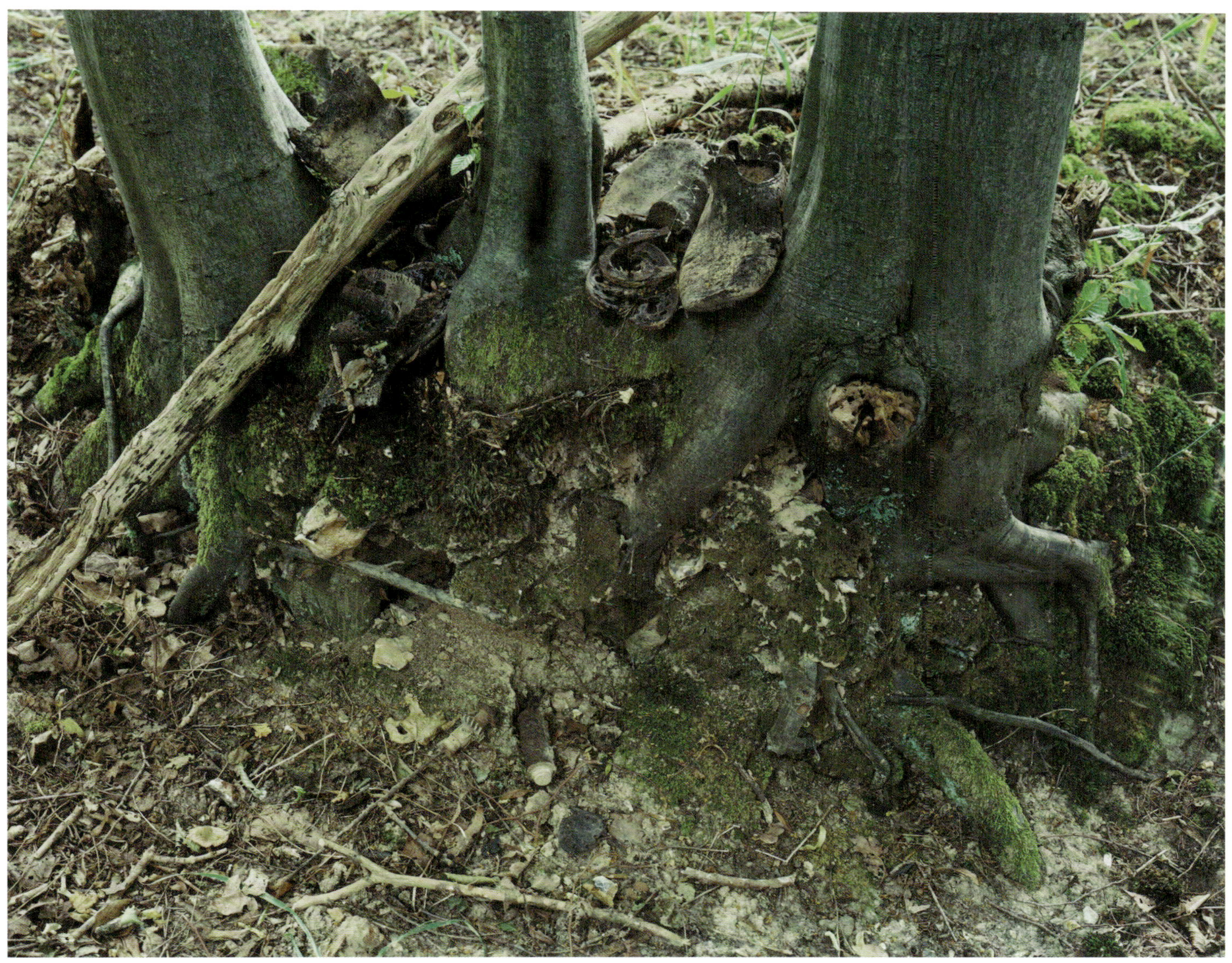

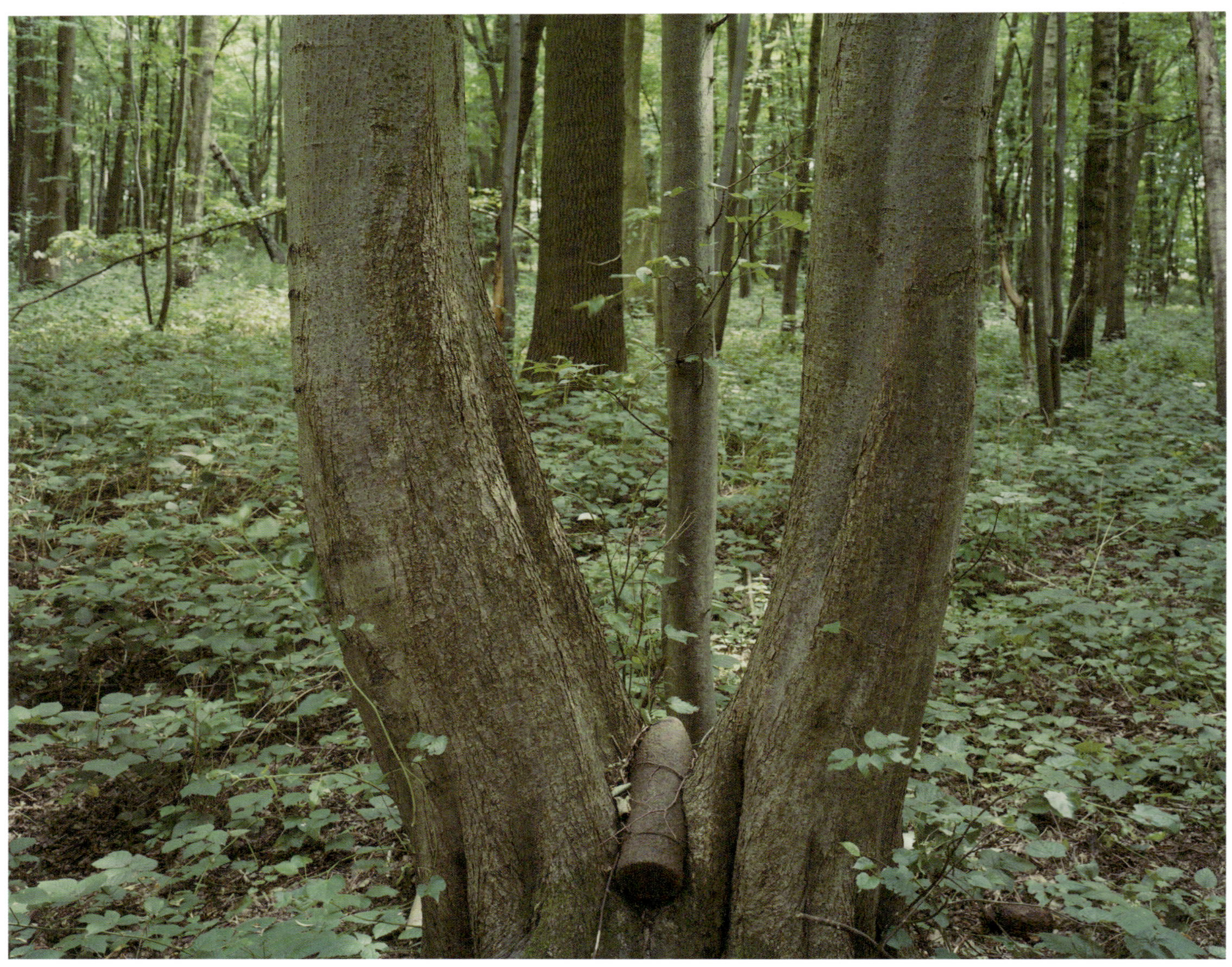

TWILIGHT

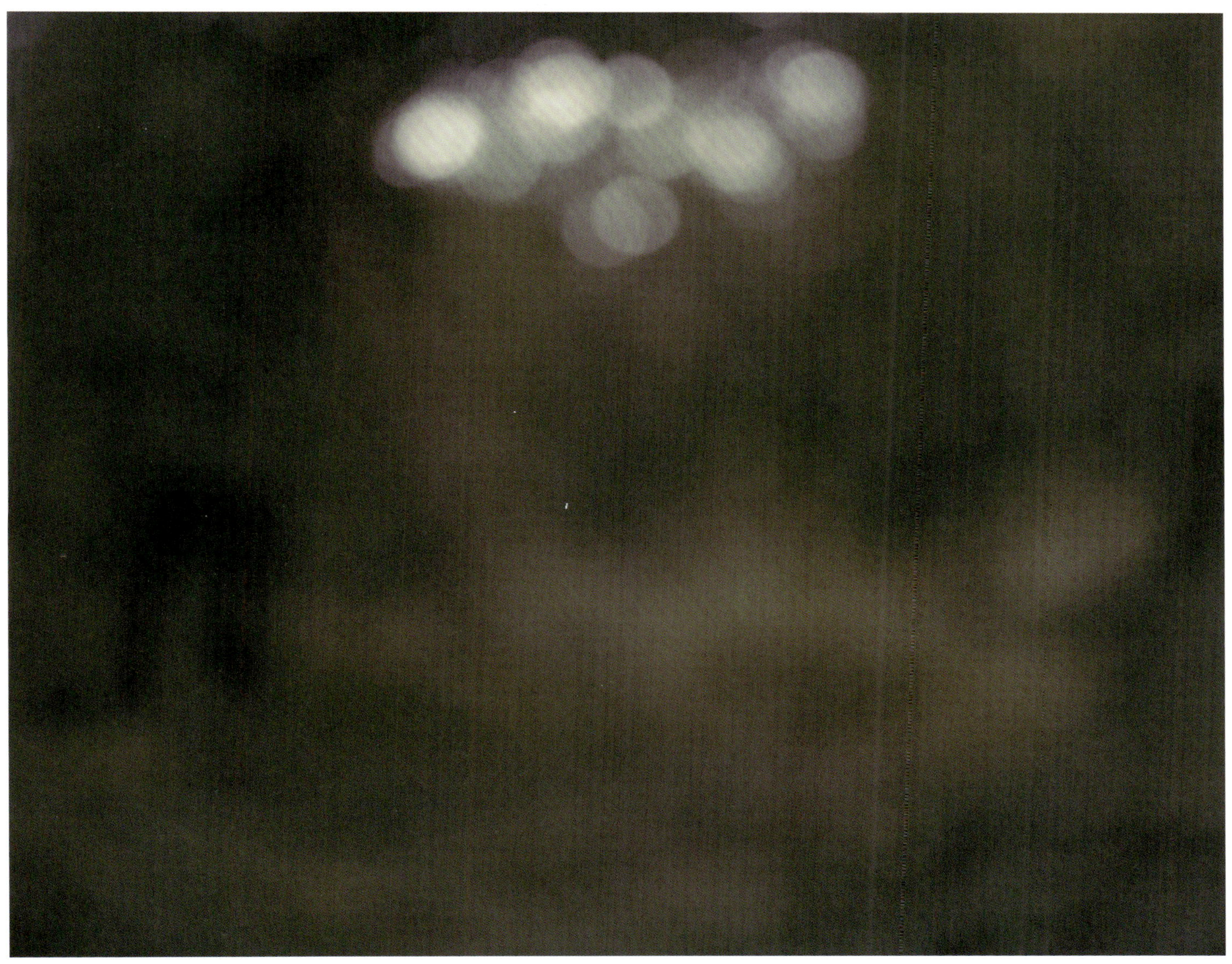

THE WOOD

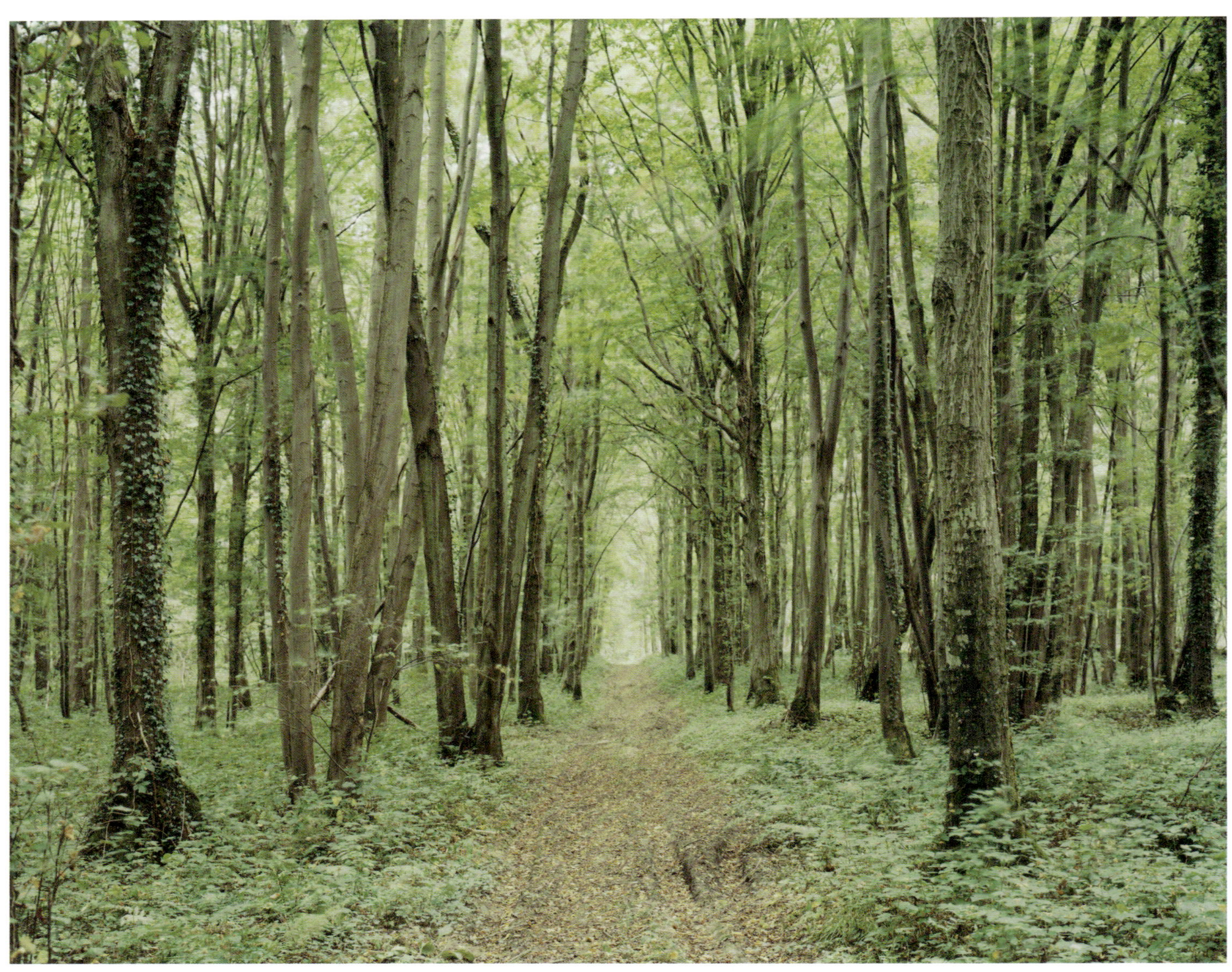

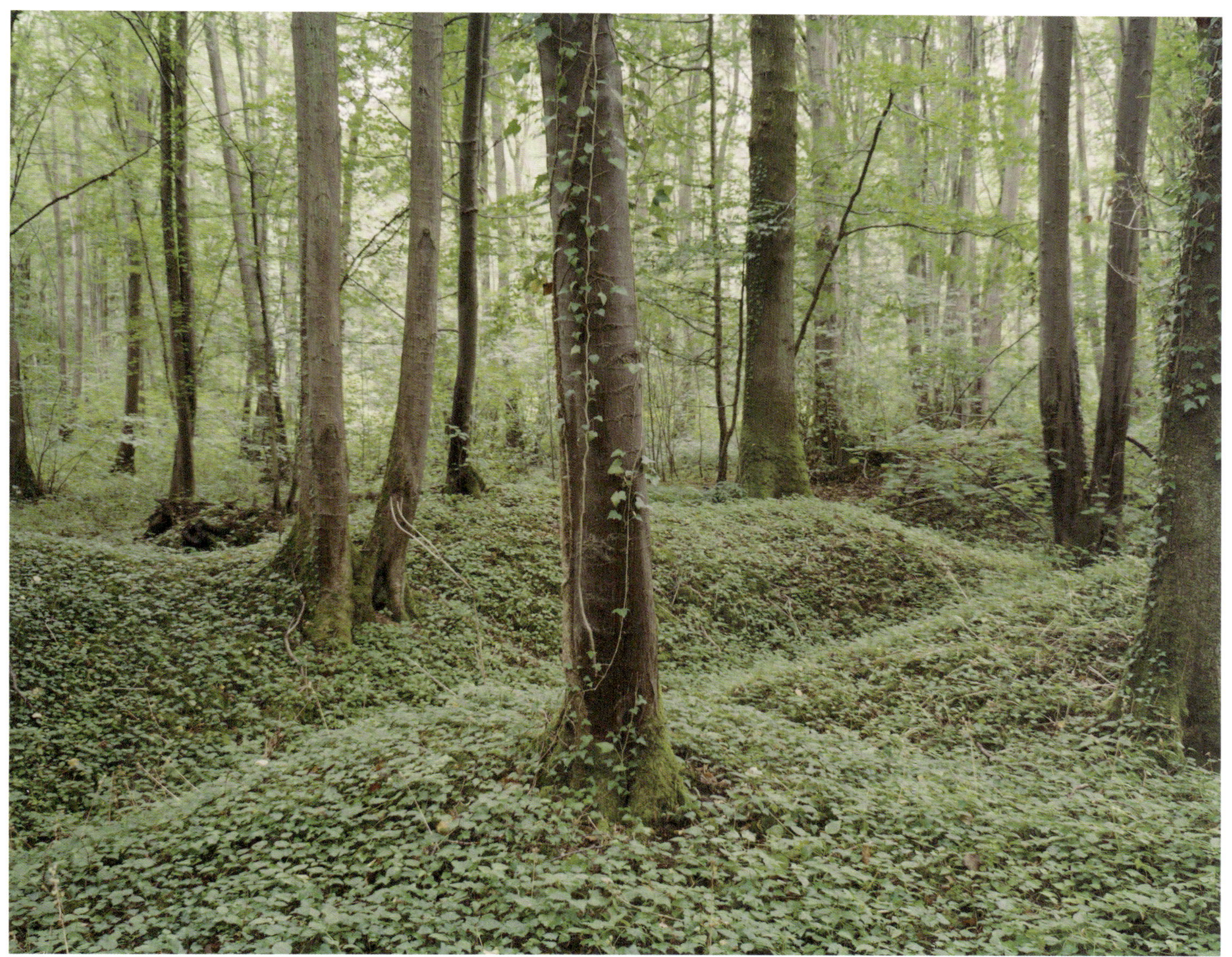

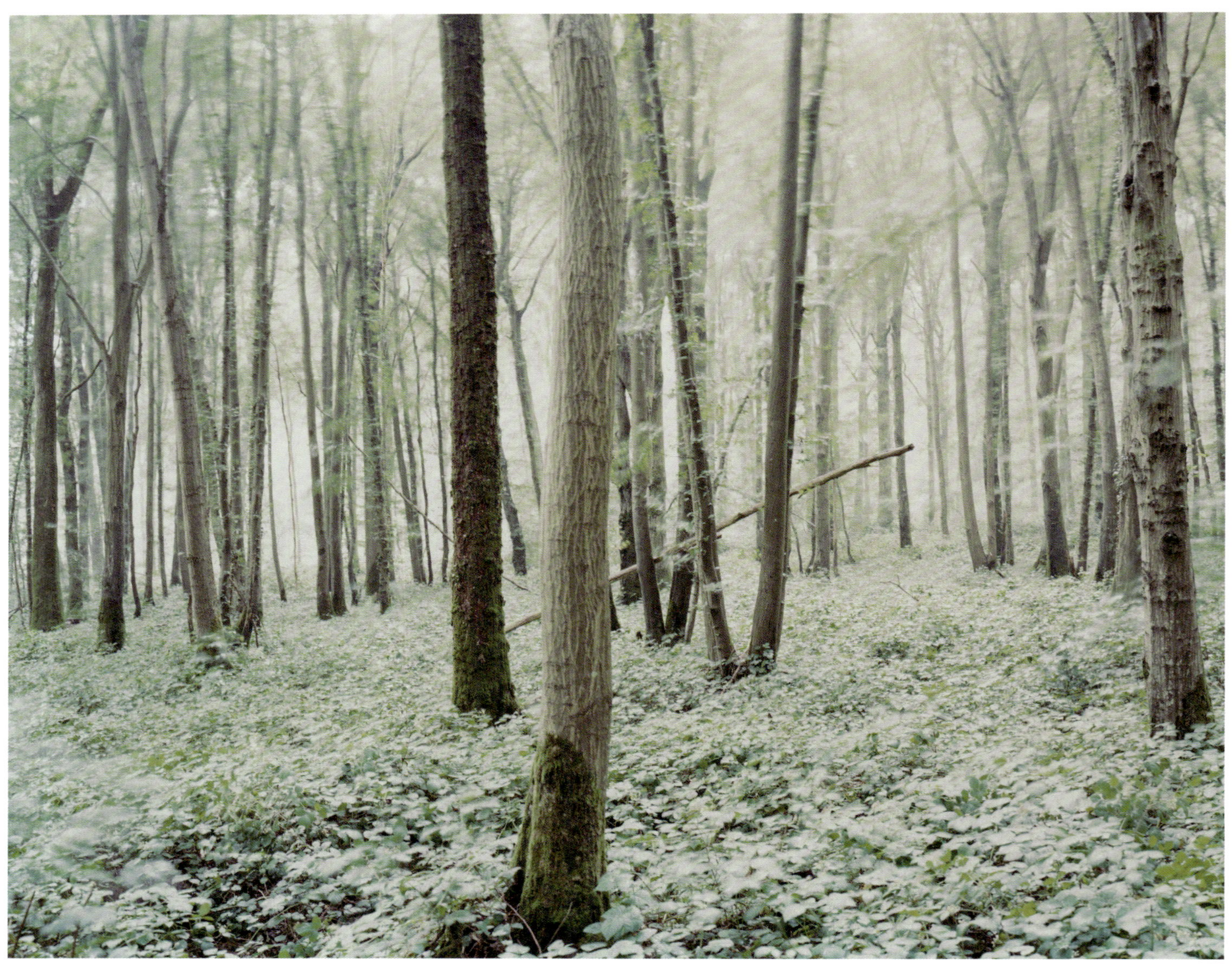

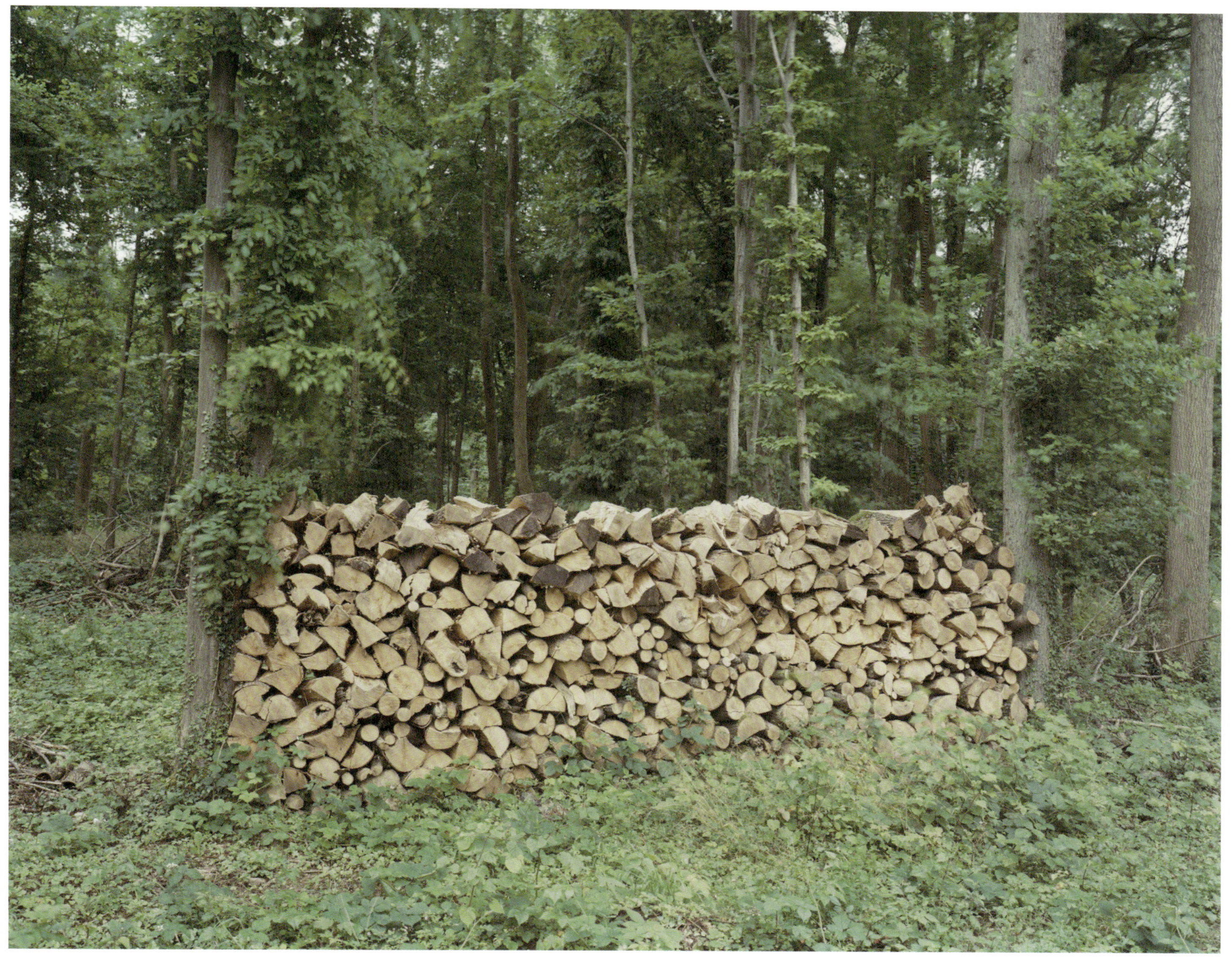

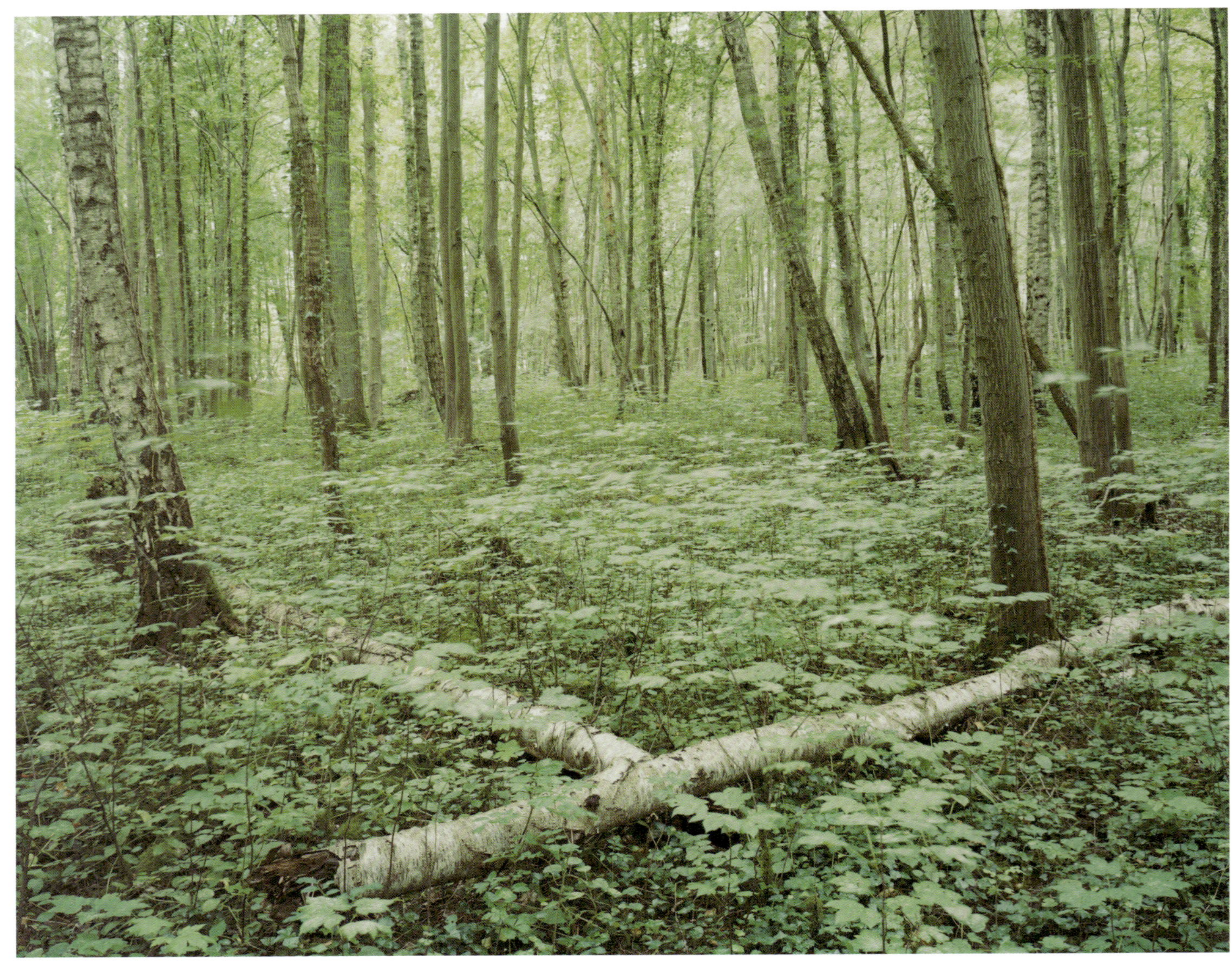

TOTEMS

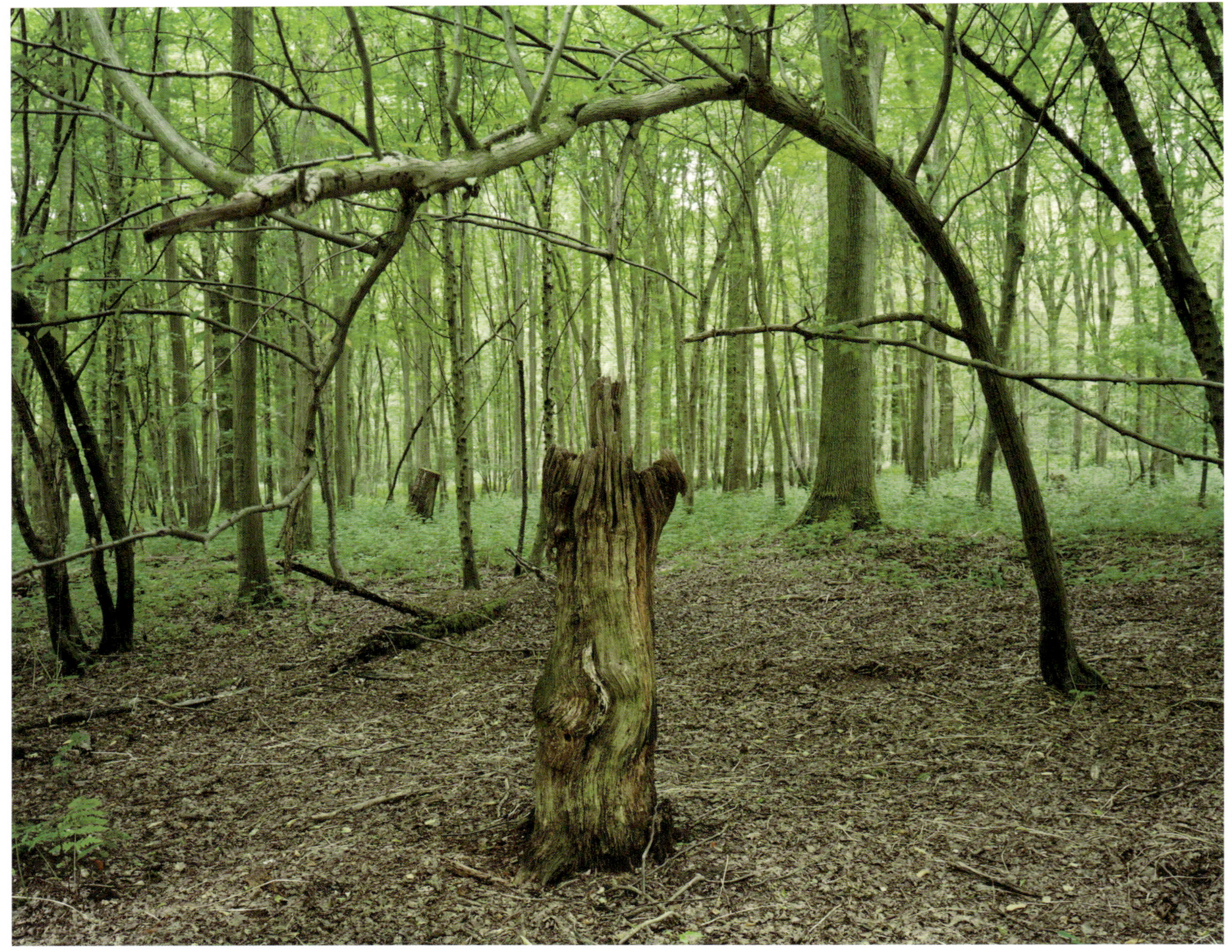

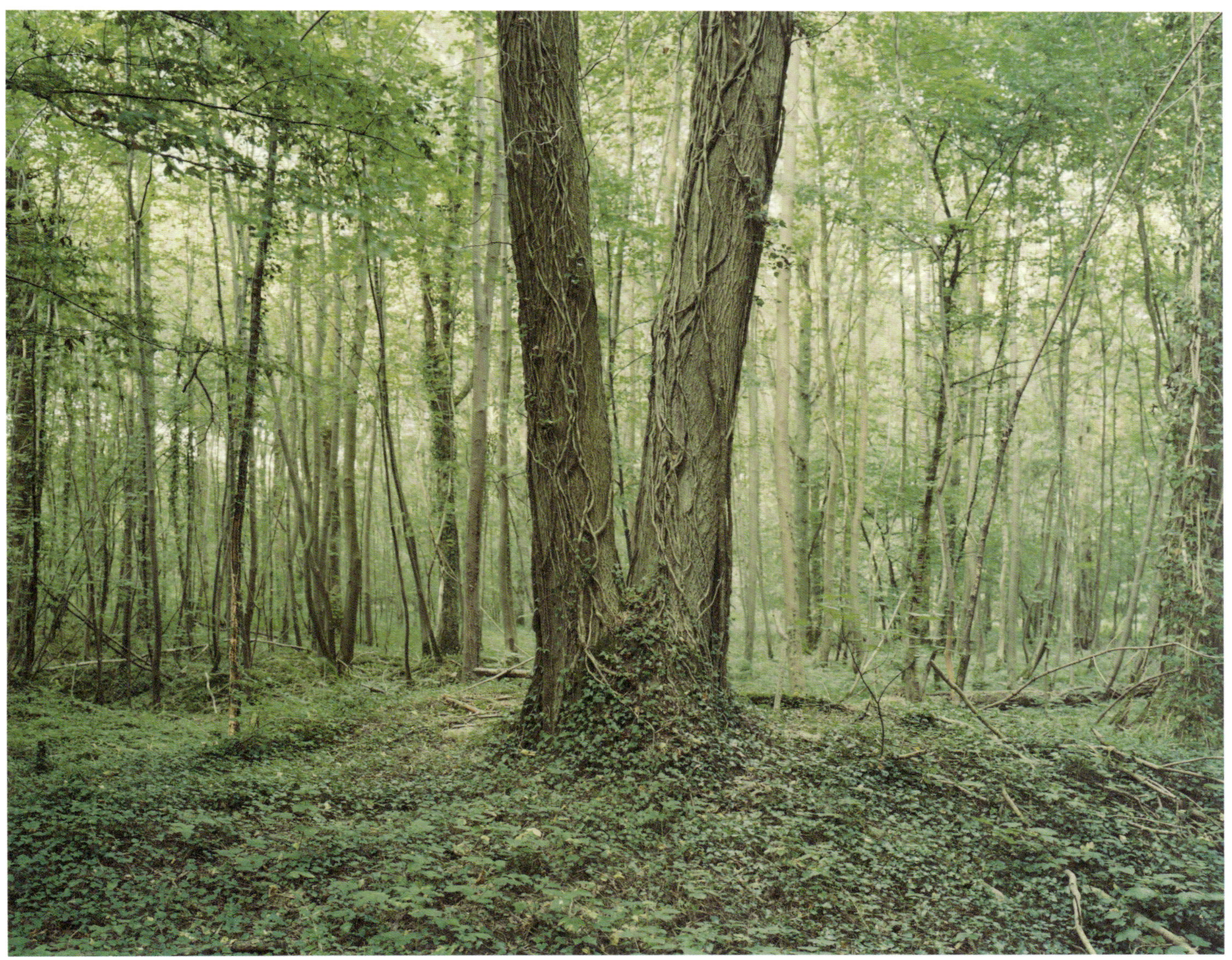

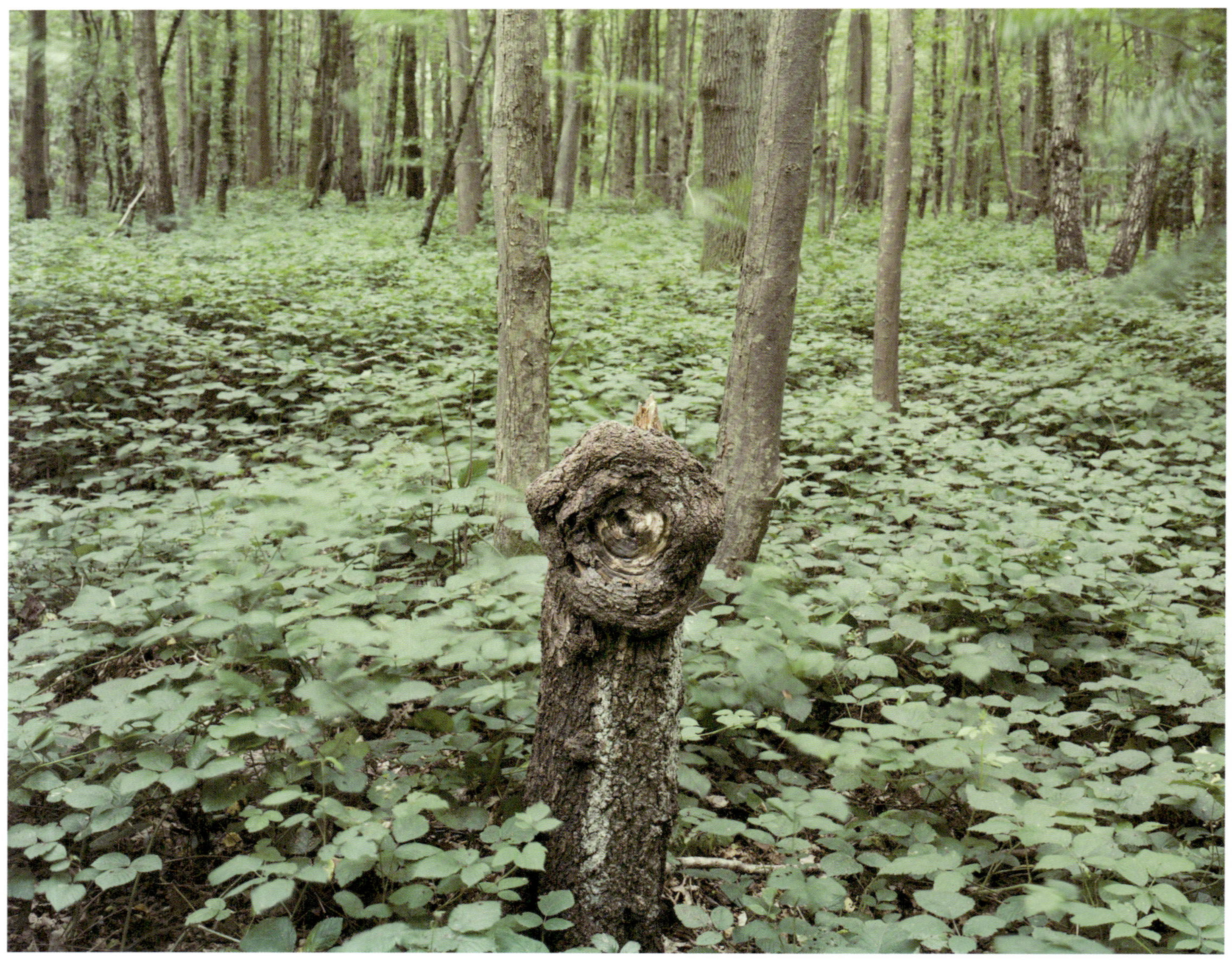

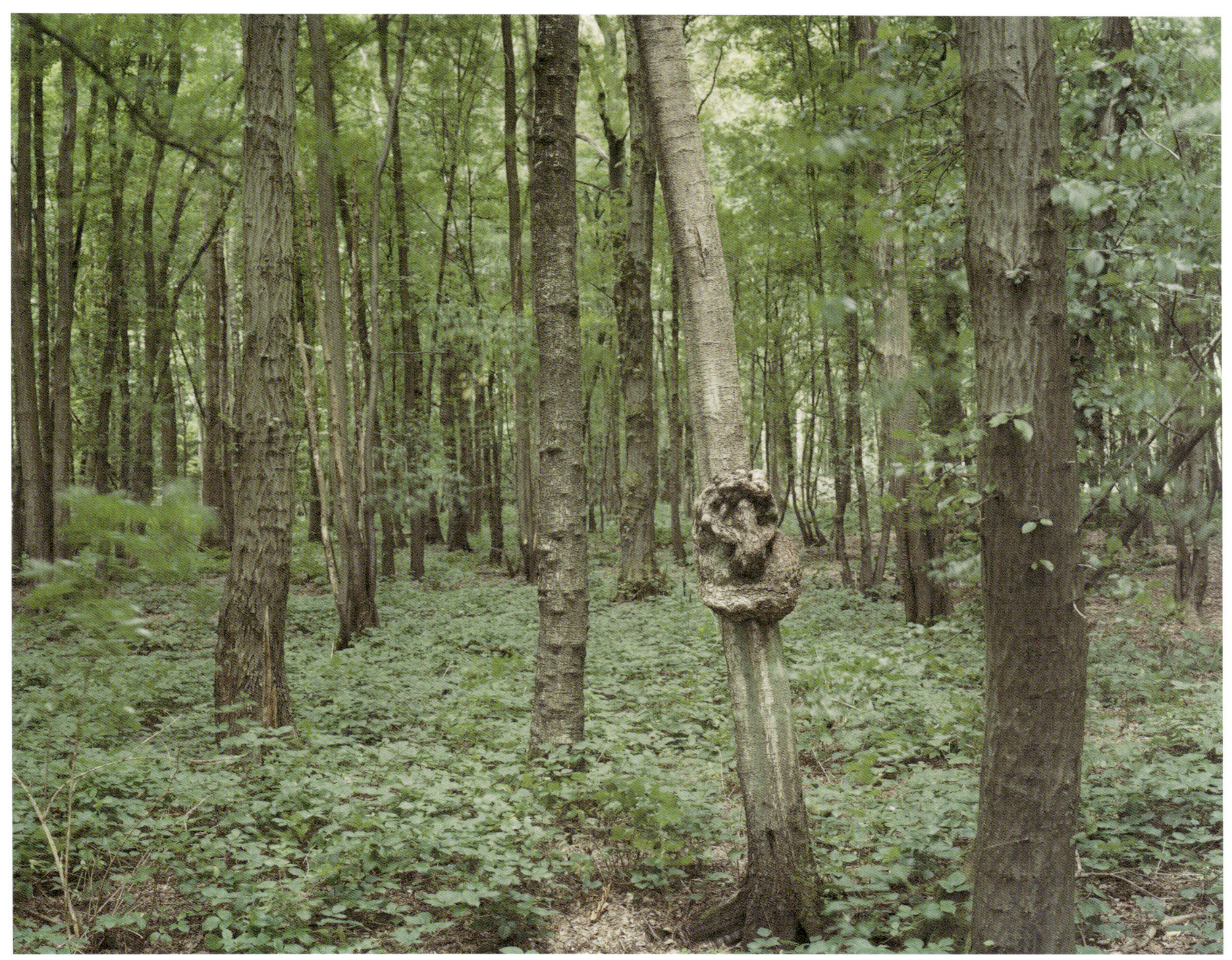

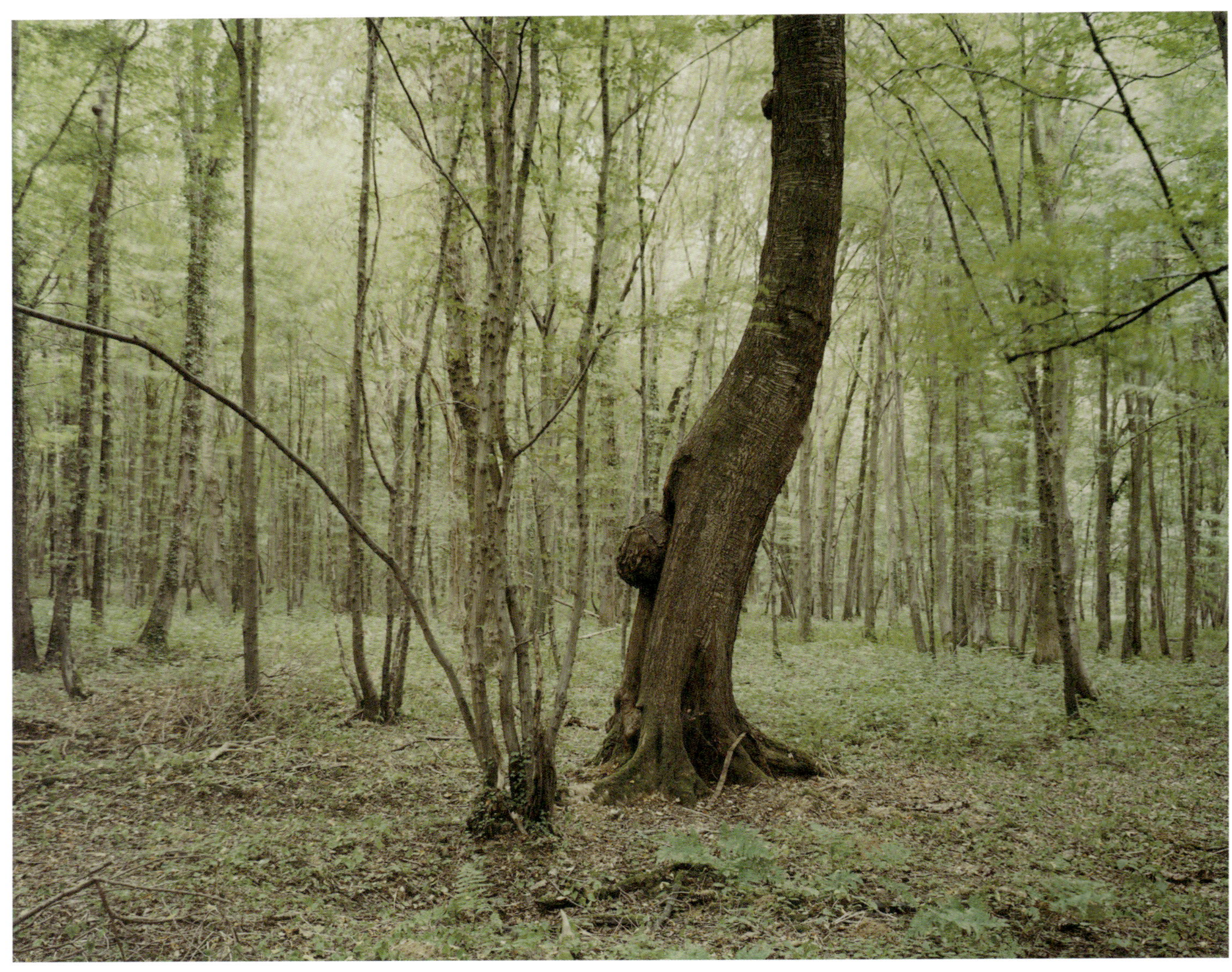

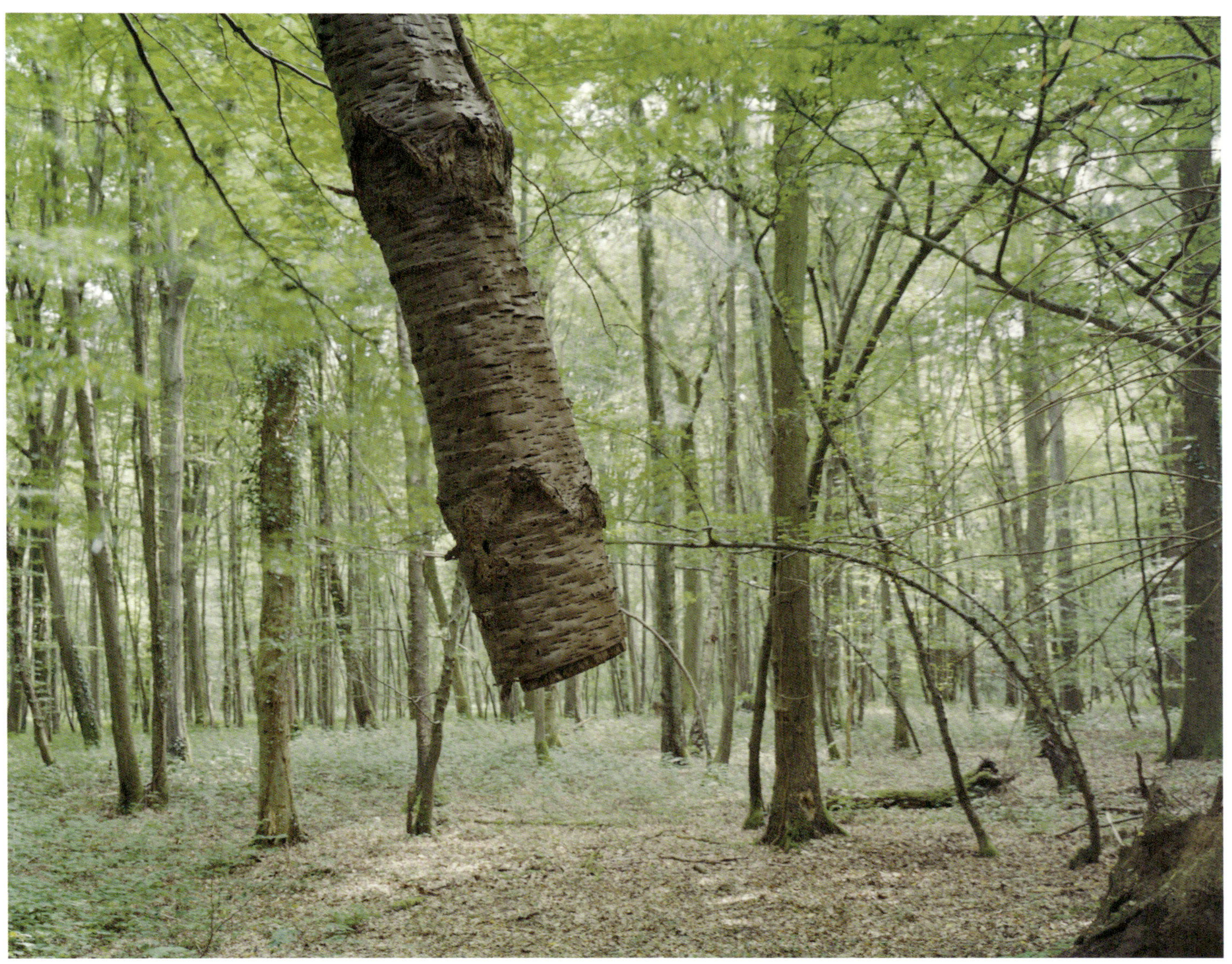

CROSSES

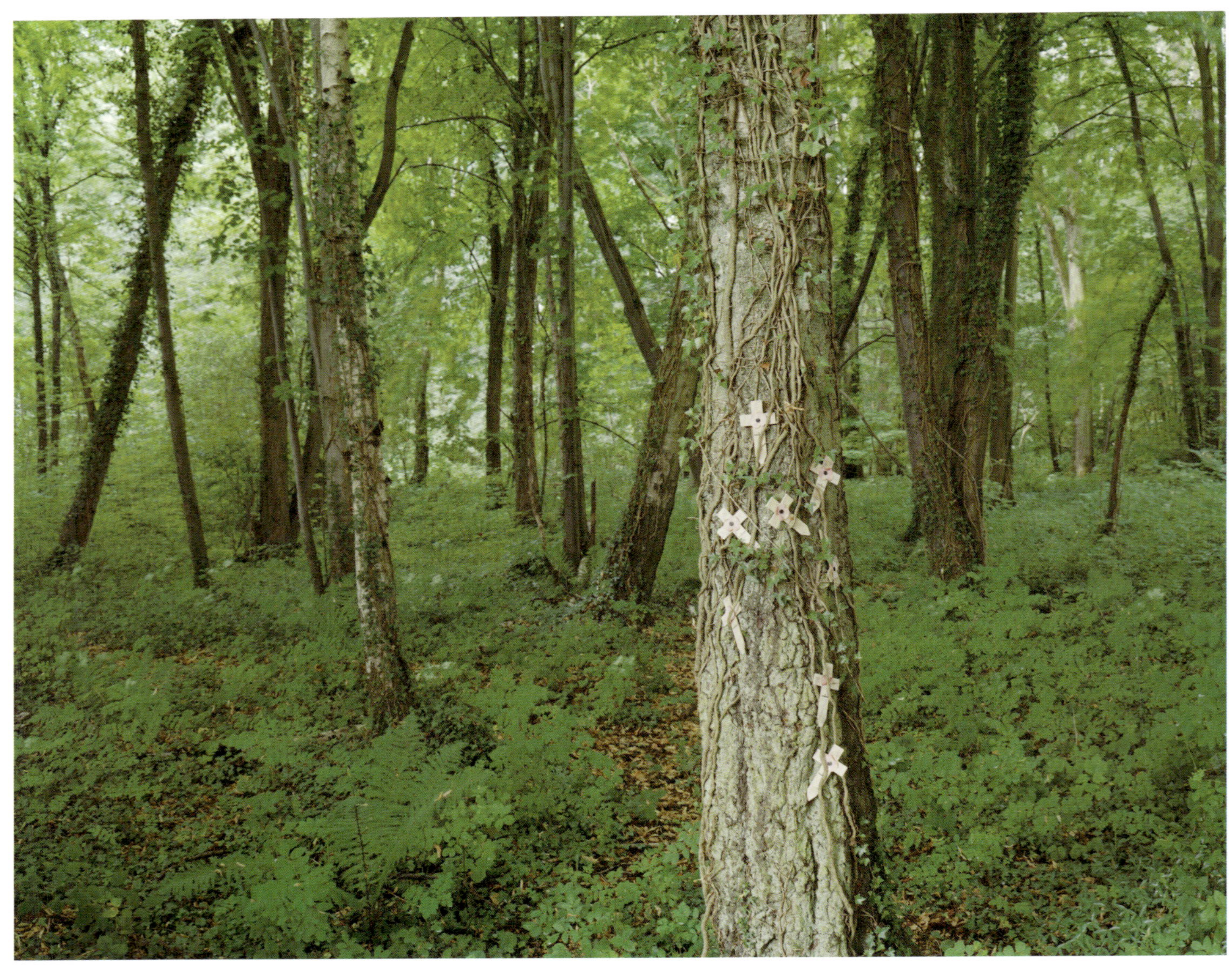

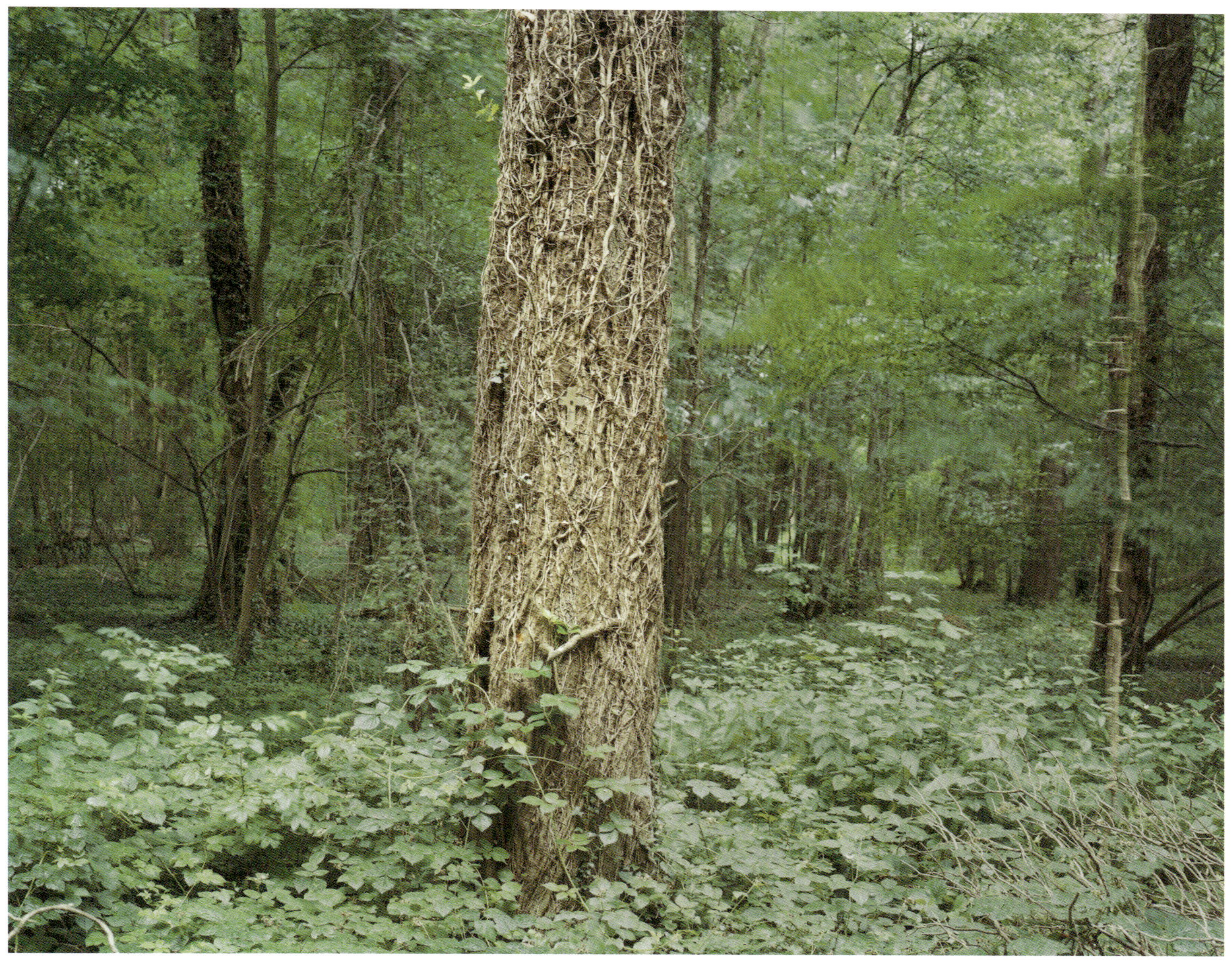

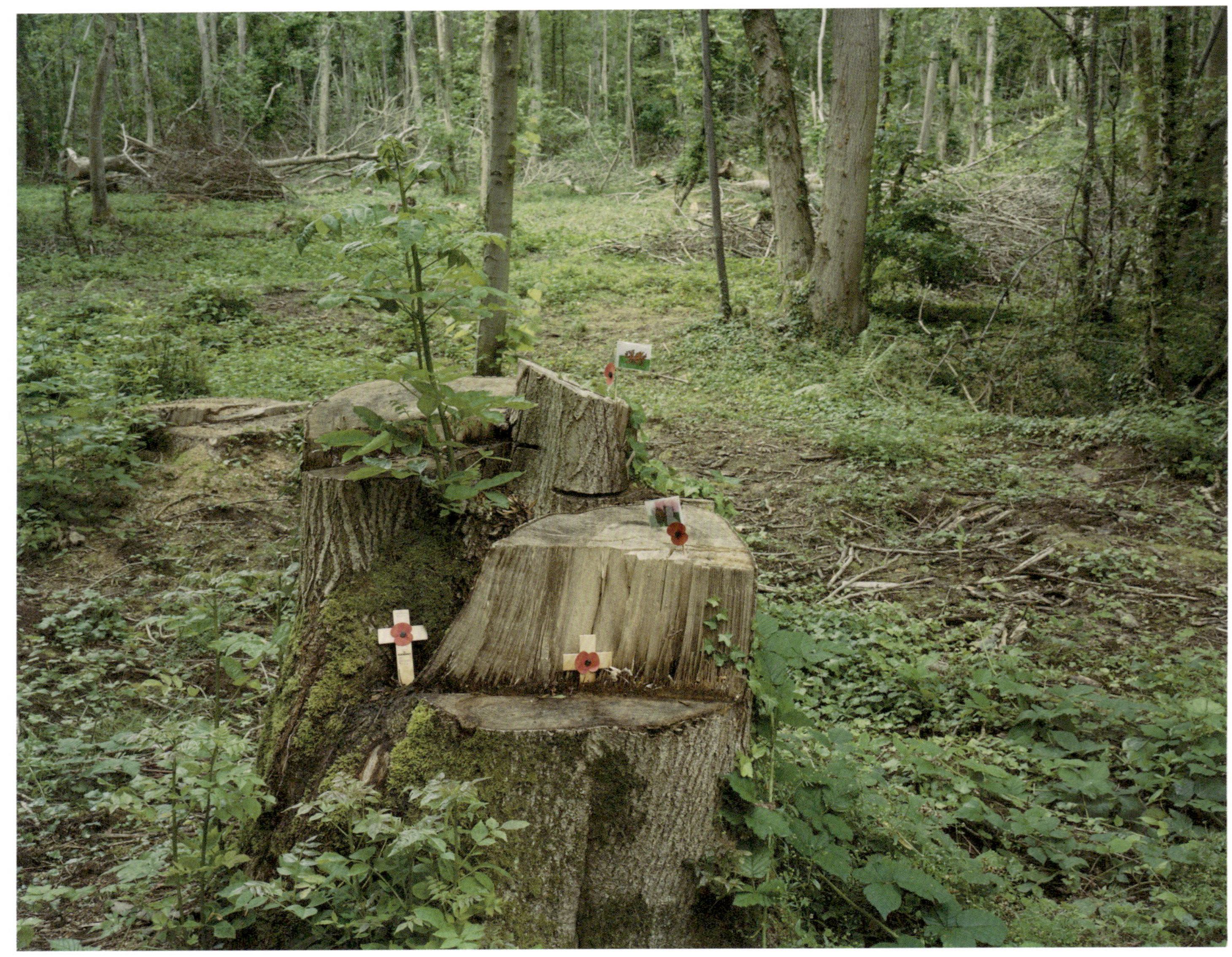

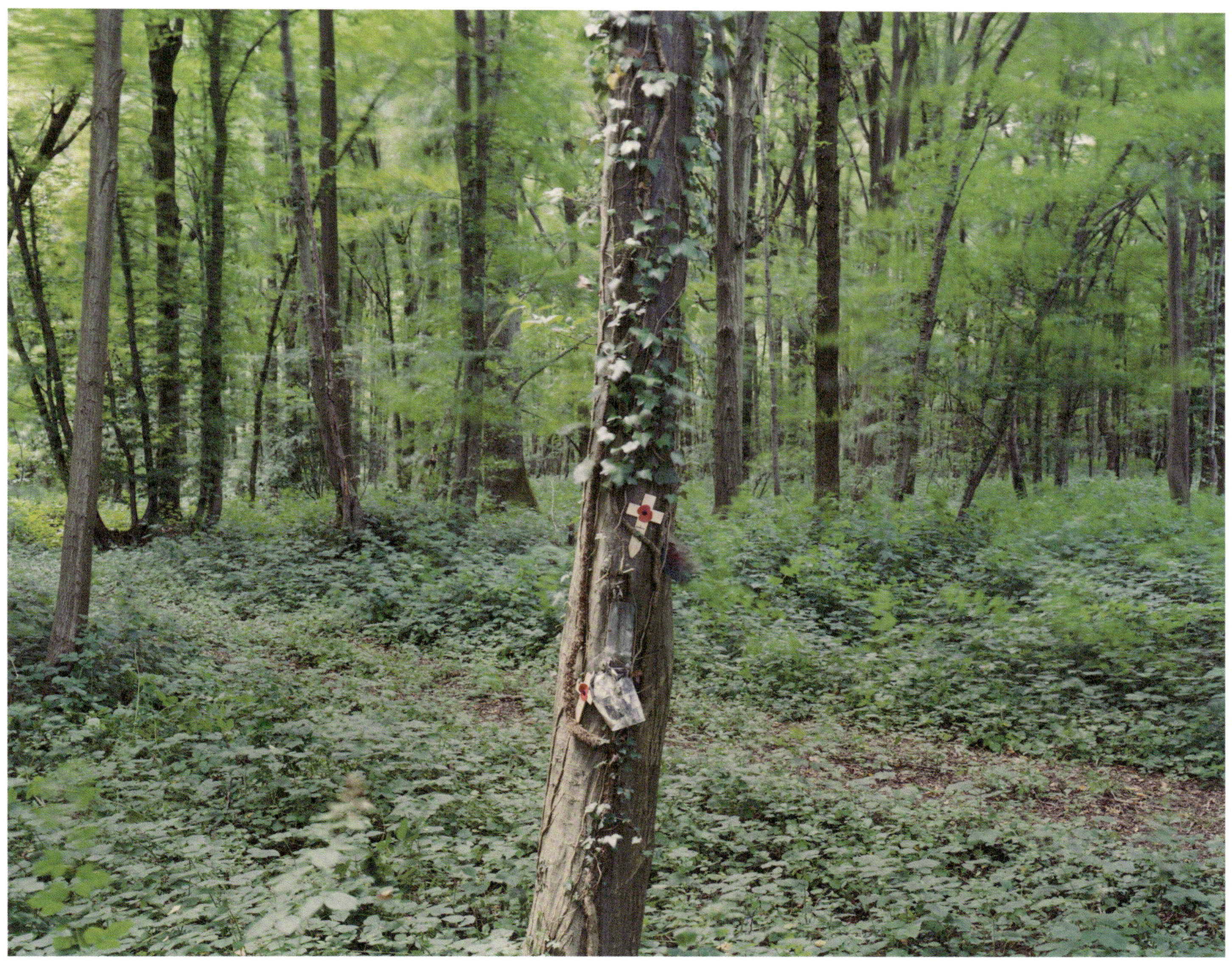

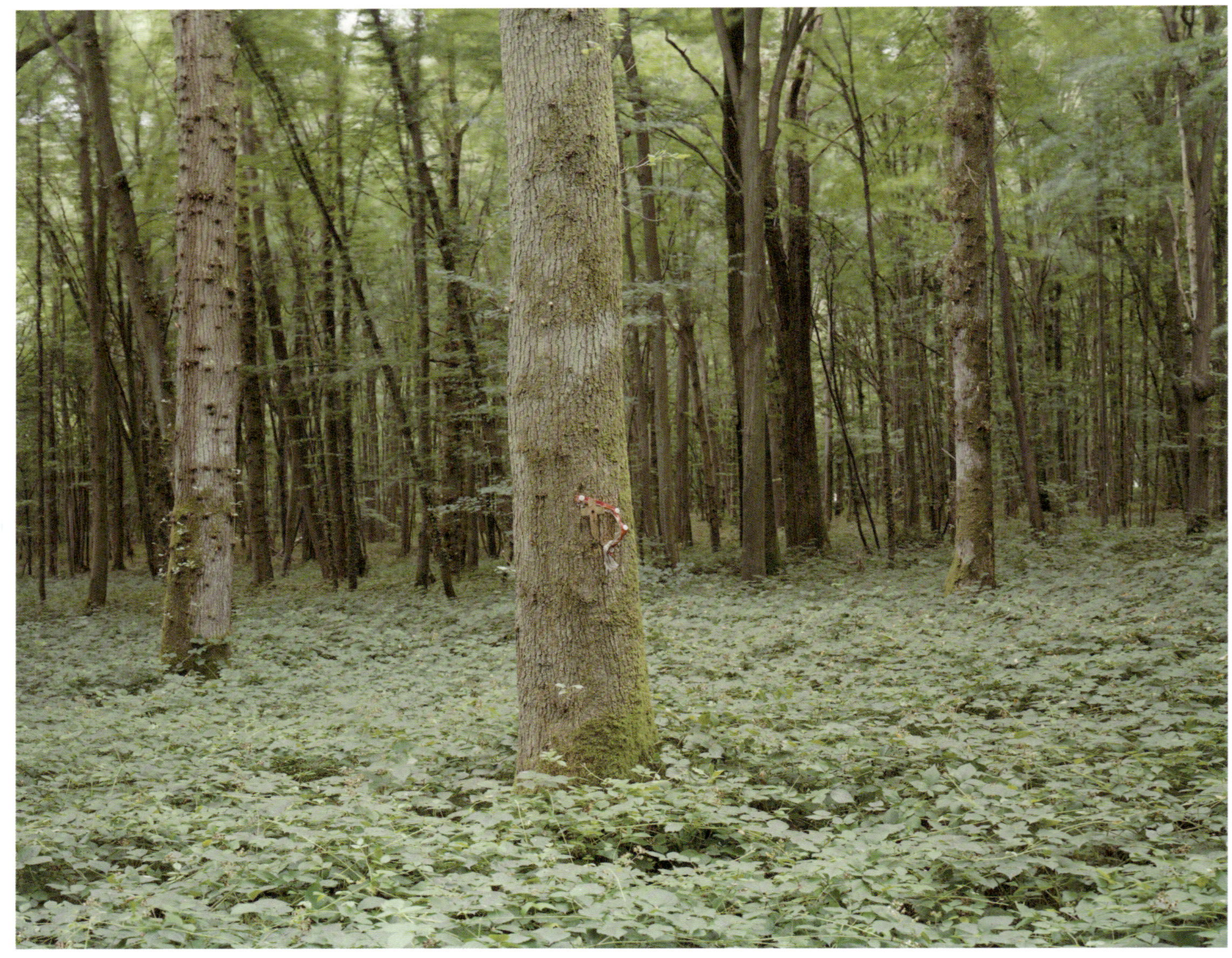

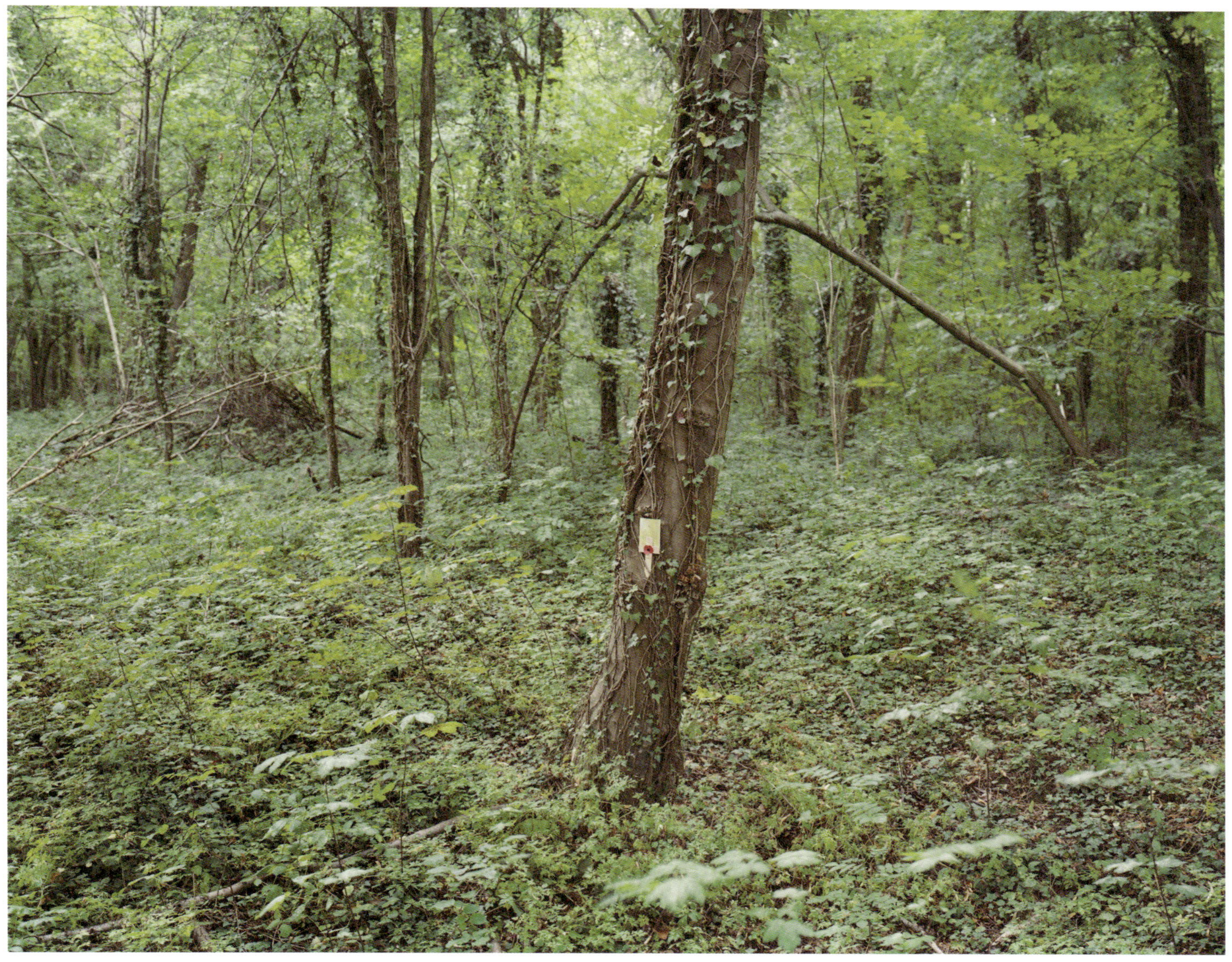

FLAGS

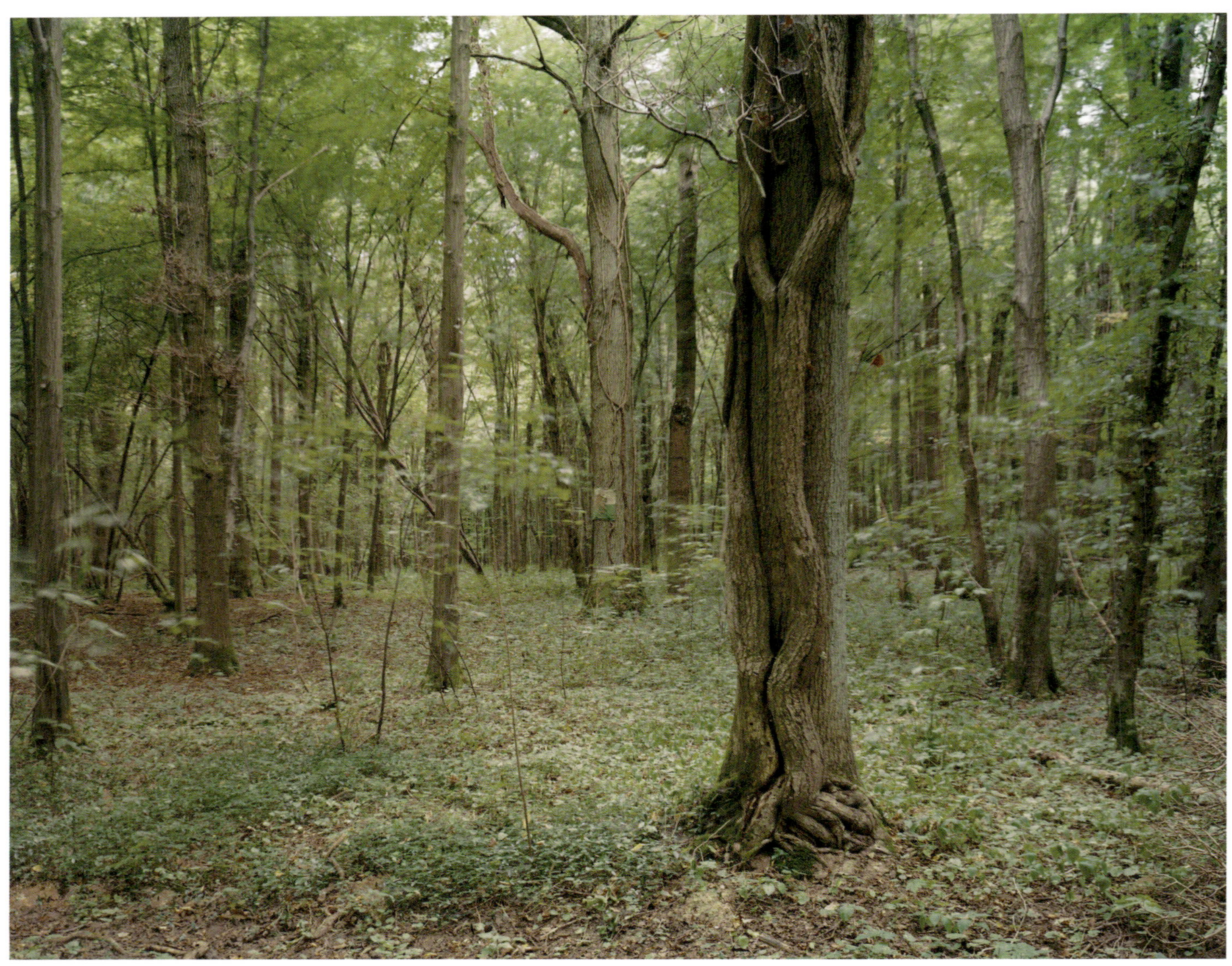

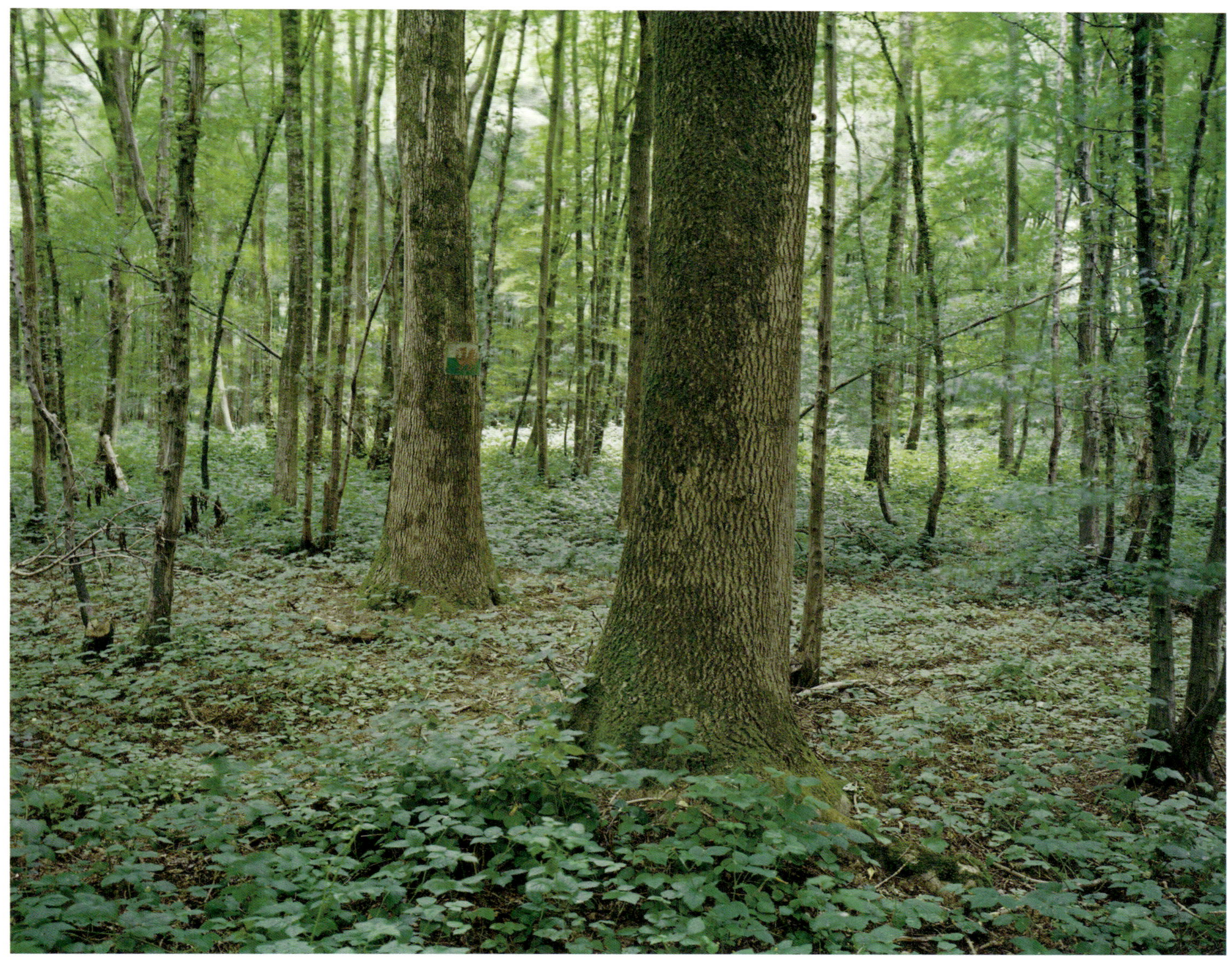

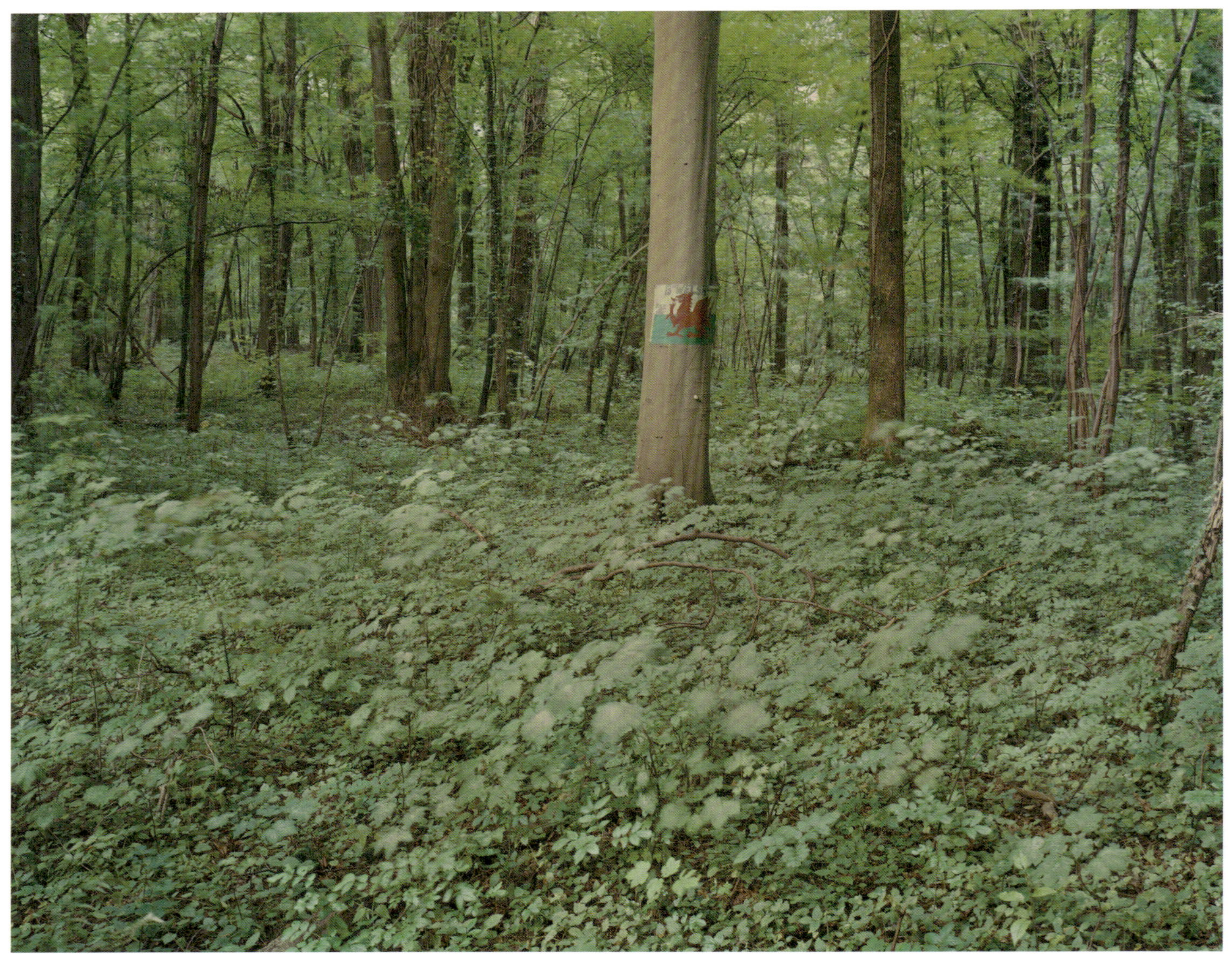

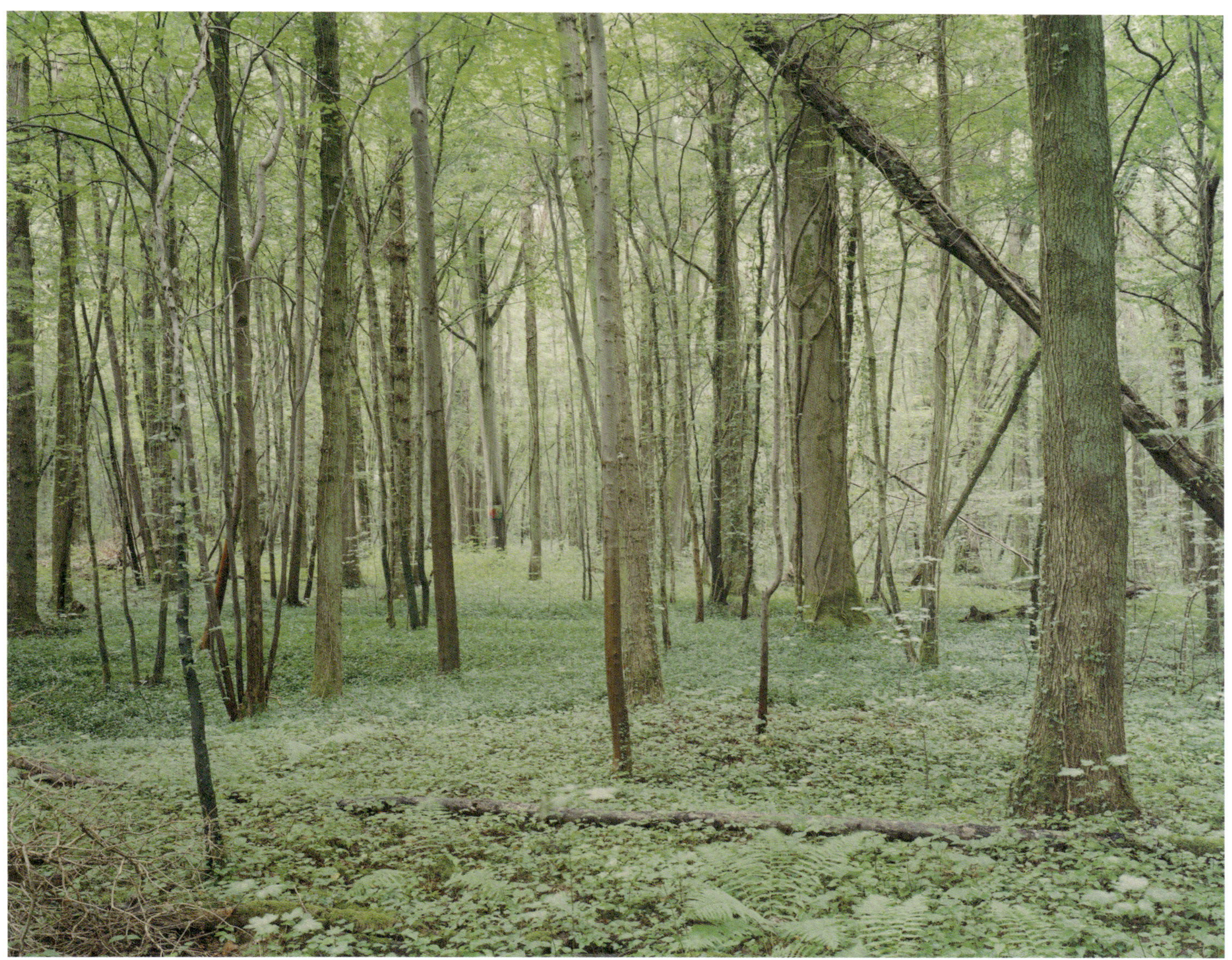

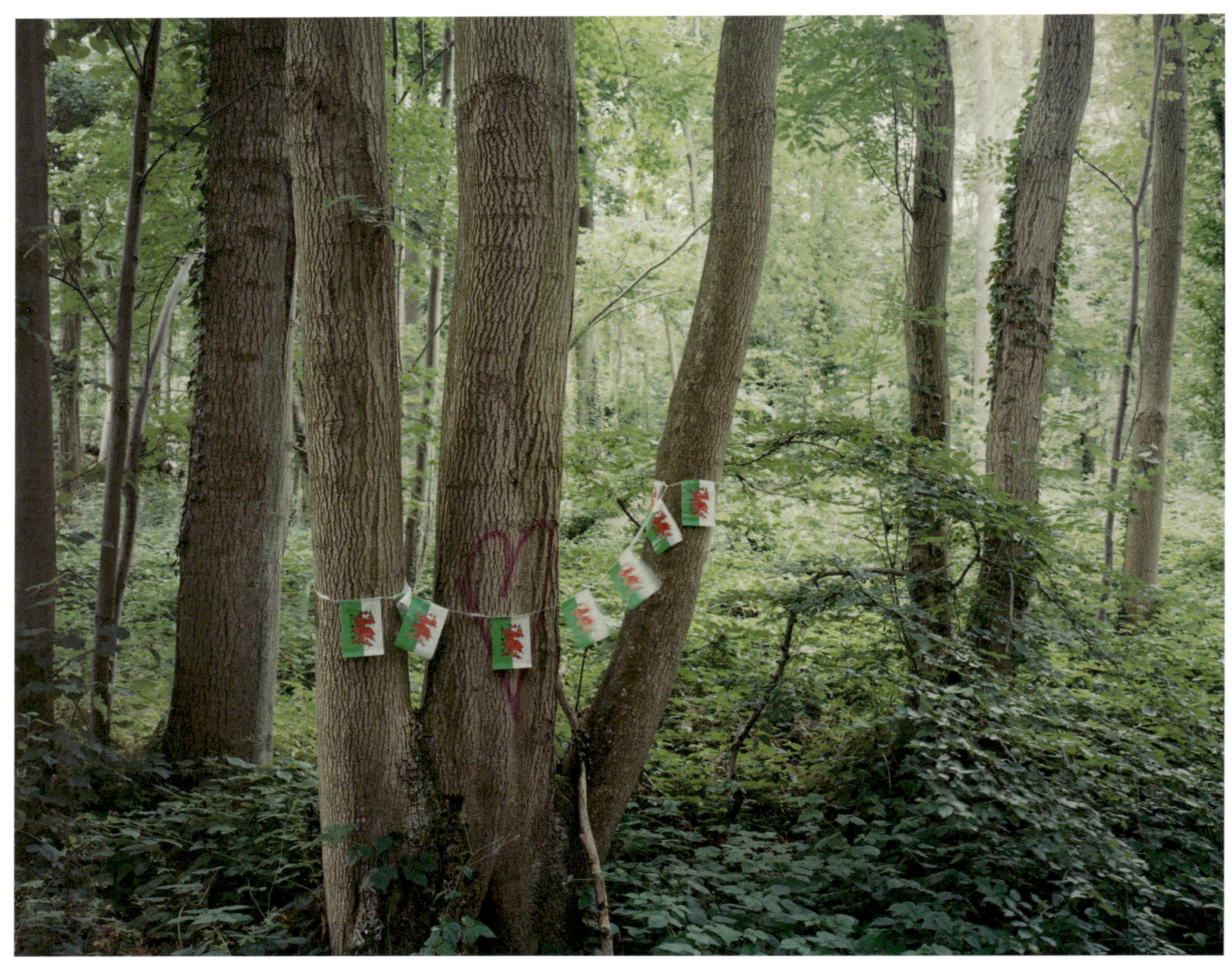

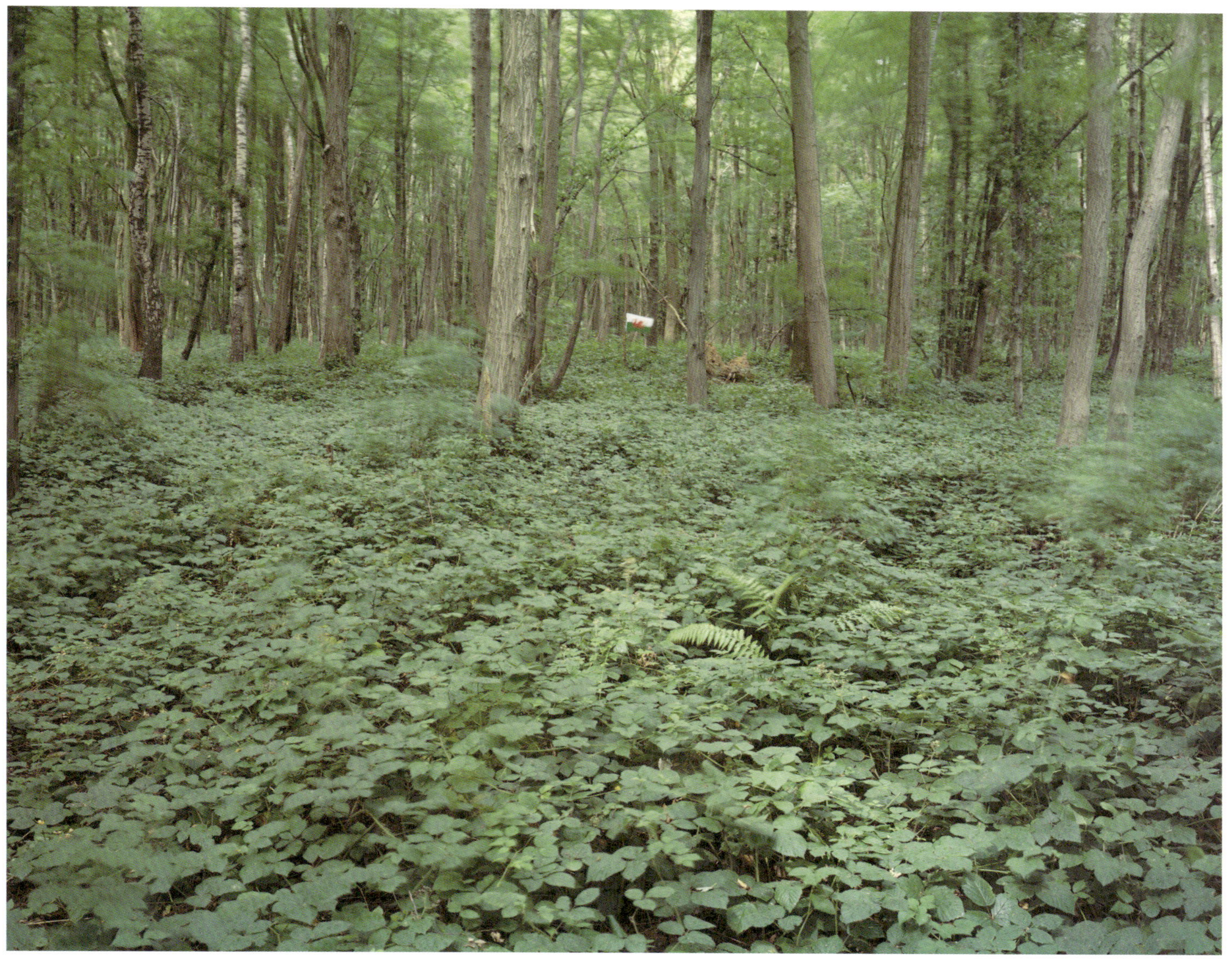

OBJECTS

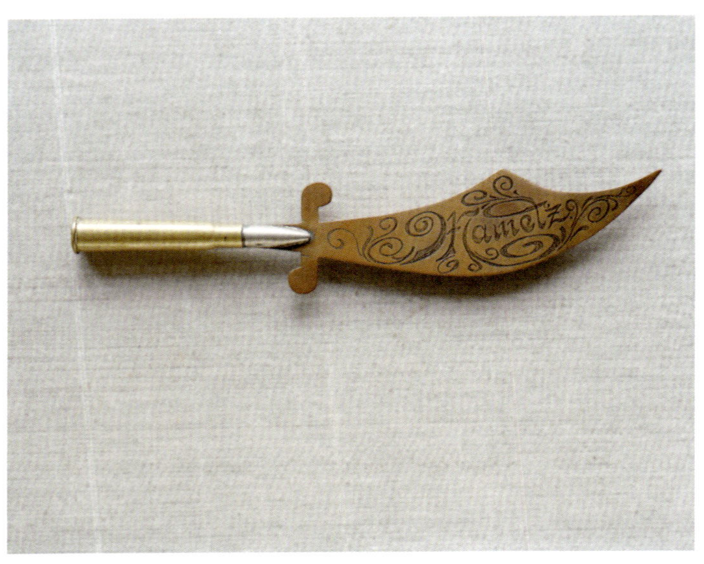

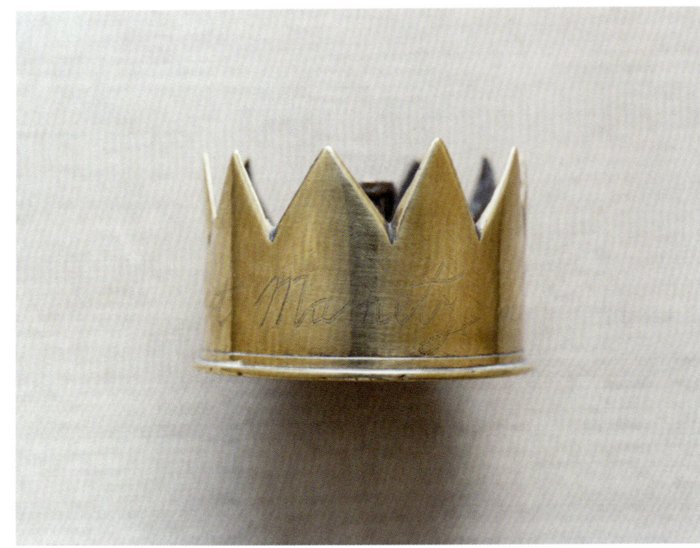

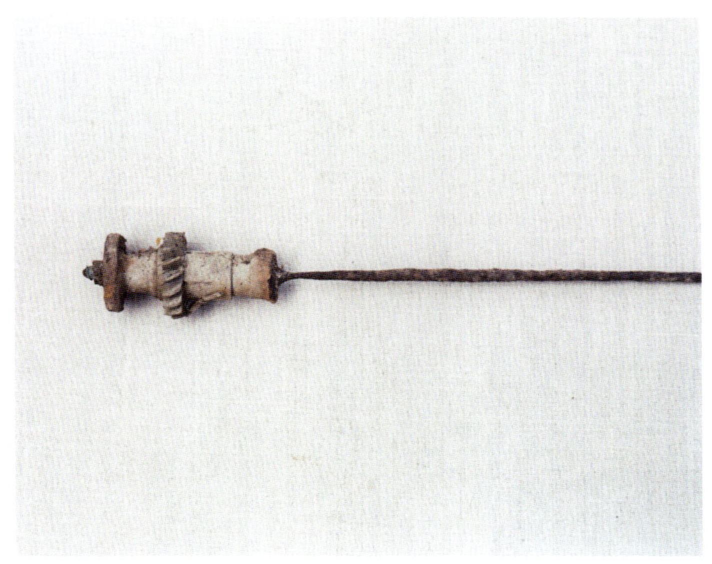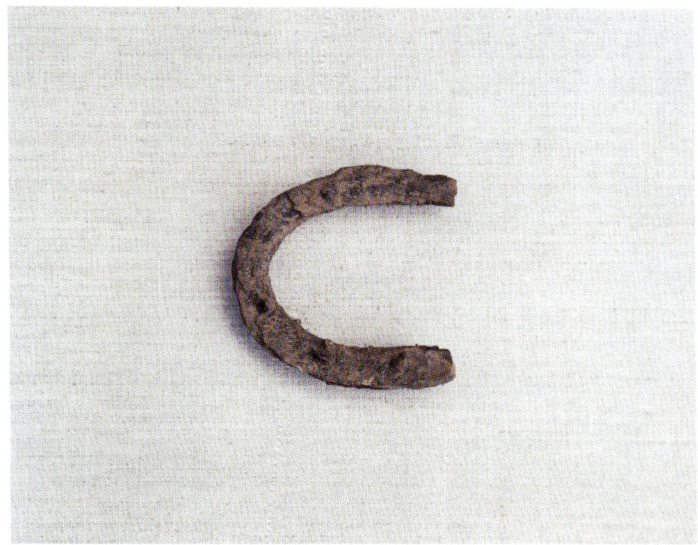

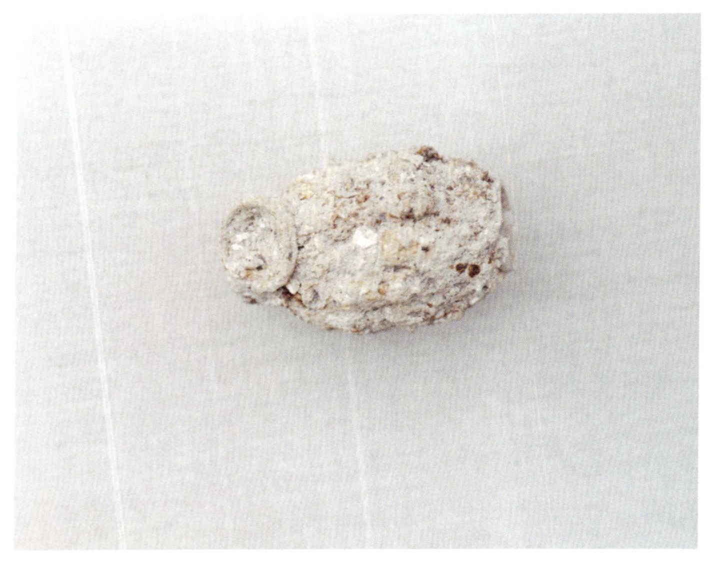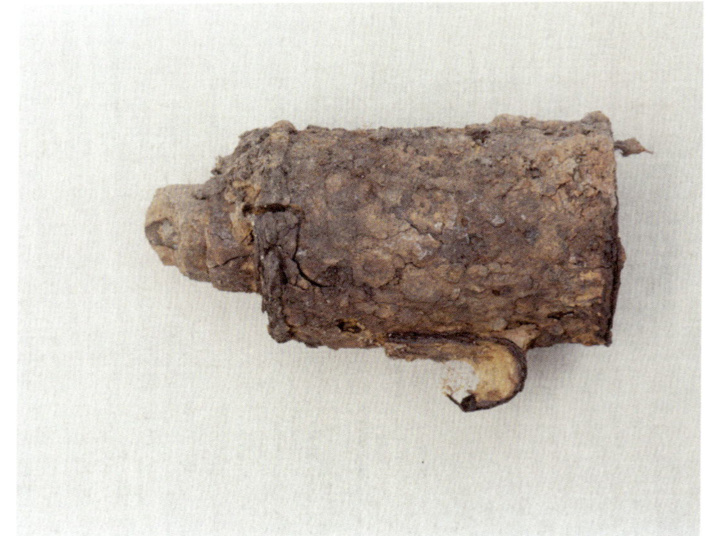

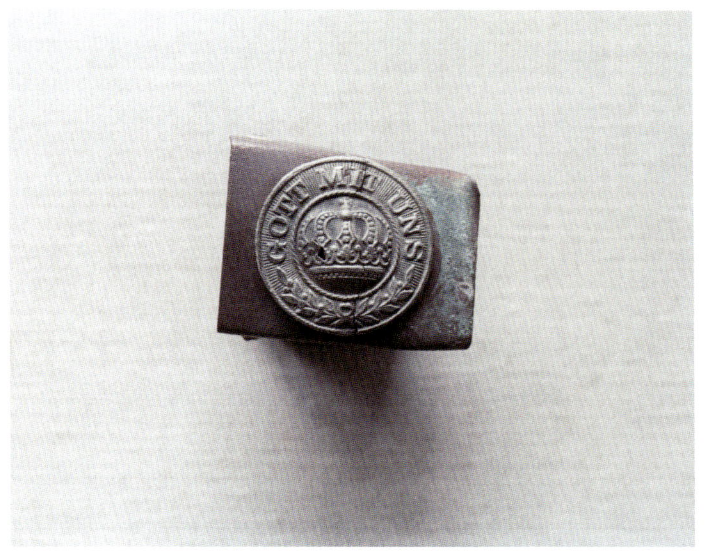

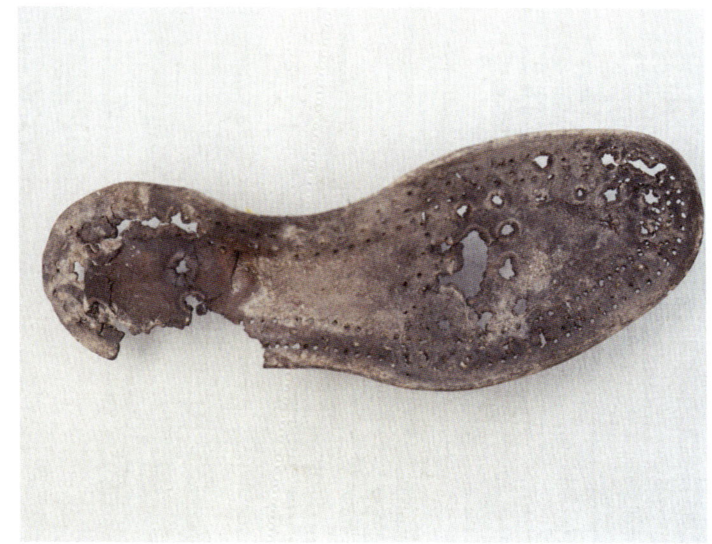

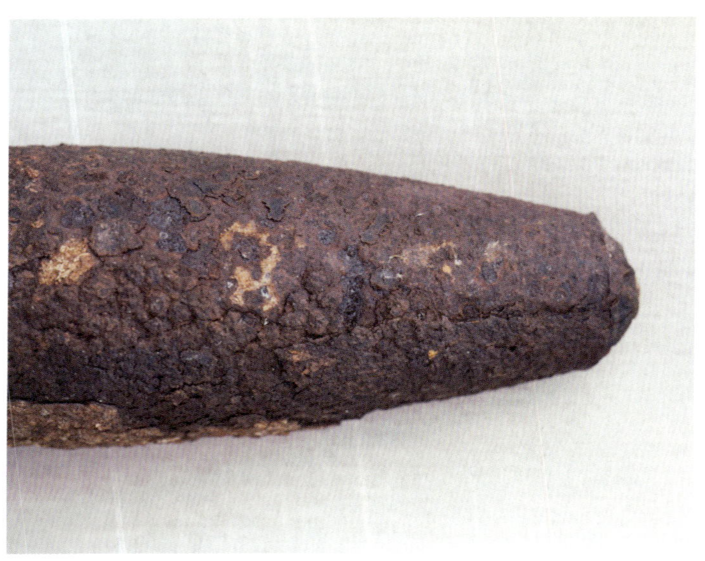
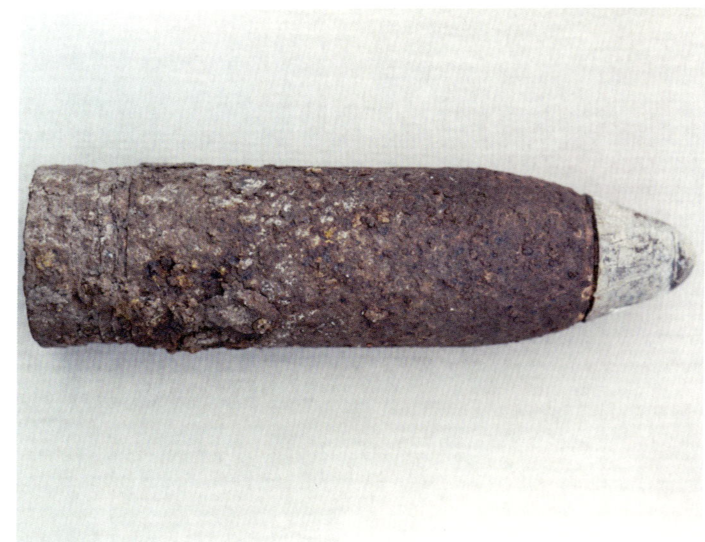

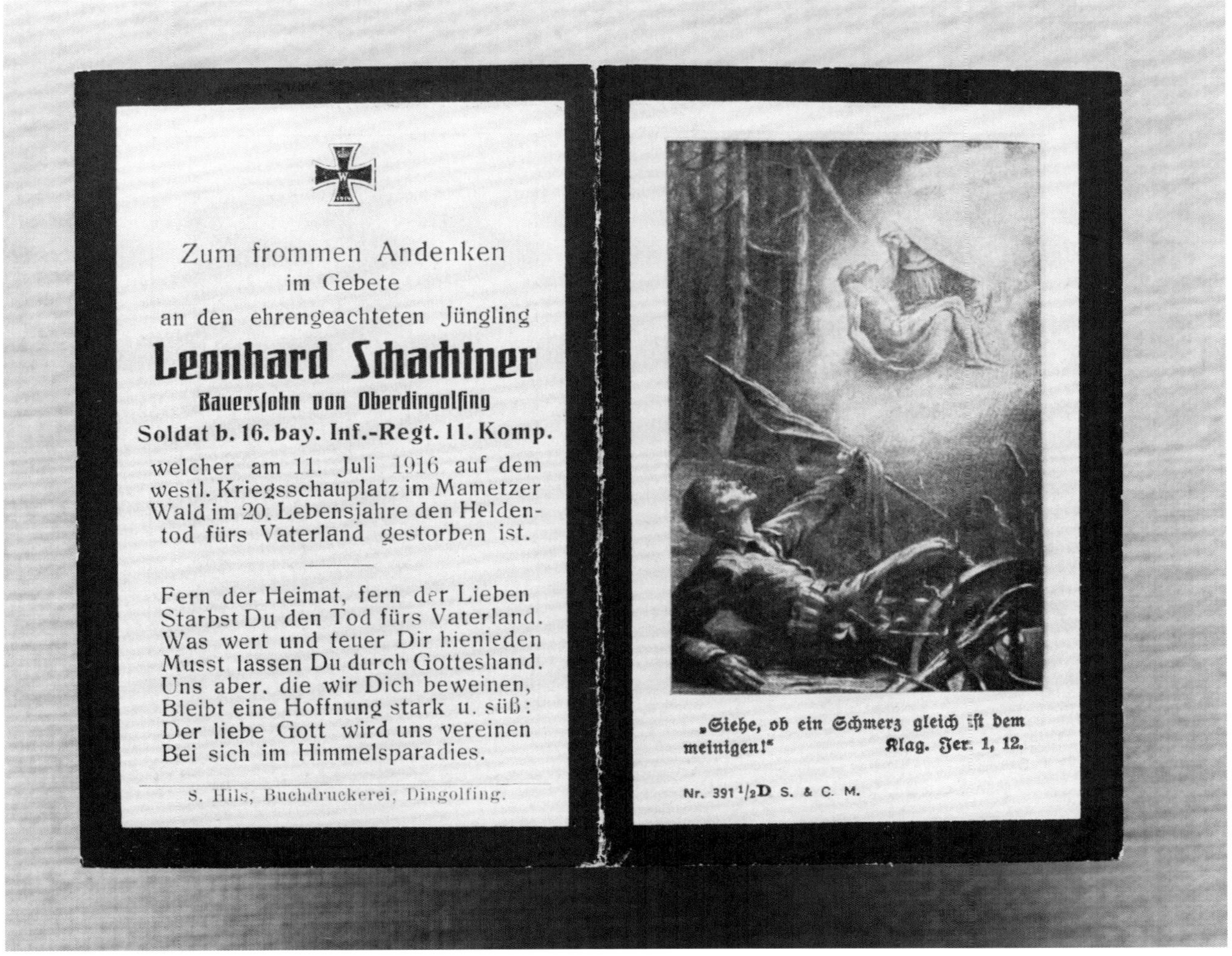

Zum frommen Andenken
im Gebete
an den ehrengeachteten Jüngling

Leonhard Schachtner
Bauersfohn von Oberdingolfing
Soldat b. 16. bay. Inf.-Regt. 11. Komp.

welcher am 11. Juli 1916 auf dem
westl. Kriegsschauplatz im Mametzer
Wald im 20. Lebensjahre den Helden-
tod fürs Vaterland gestorben ist.

———

Fern der Heimat, fern der Lieben
Starbst Du den Tod fürs Vaterland.
Was wert und teuer Dir hienieden
Musst lassen Du durch Gotteshand.
Uns aber, die wir Dich beweinen,
Bleibt eine Hoffnung stark u. süß:
Der liebe Gott wird uns vereinen
Bei sich im Himmelsparadies.

S. Hils, Buchdruckerei, Dingolfing.

„Siehe, ob ein Schmerz gleich ist dem
meinigen!"   Klag. Jer. 1, 12.

Nr. 391 1/2 D S. & C. M.

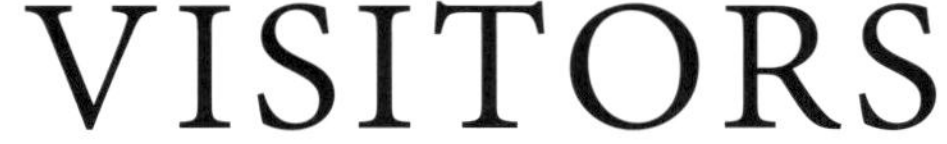
VISITORS

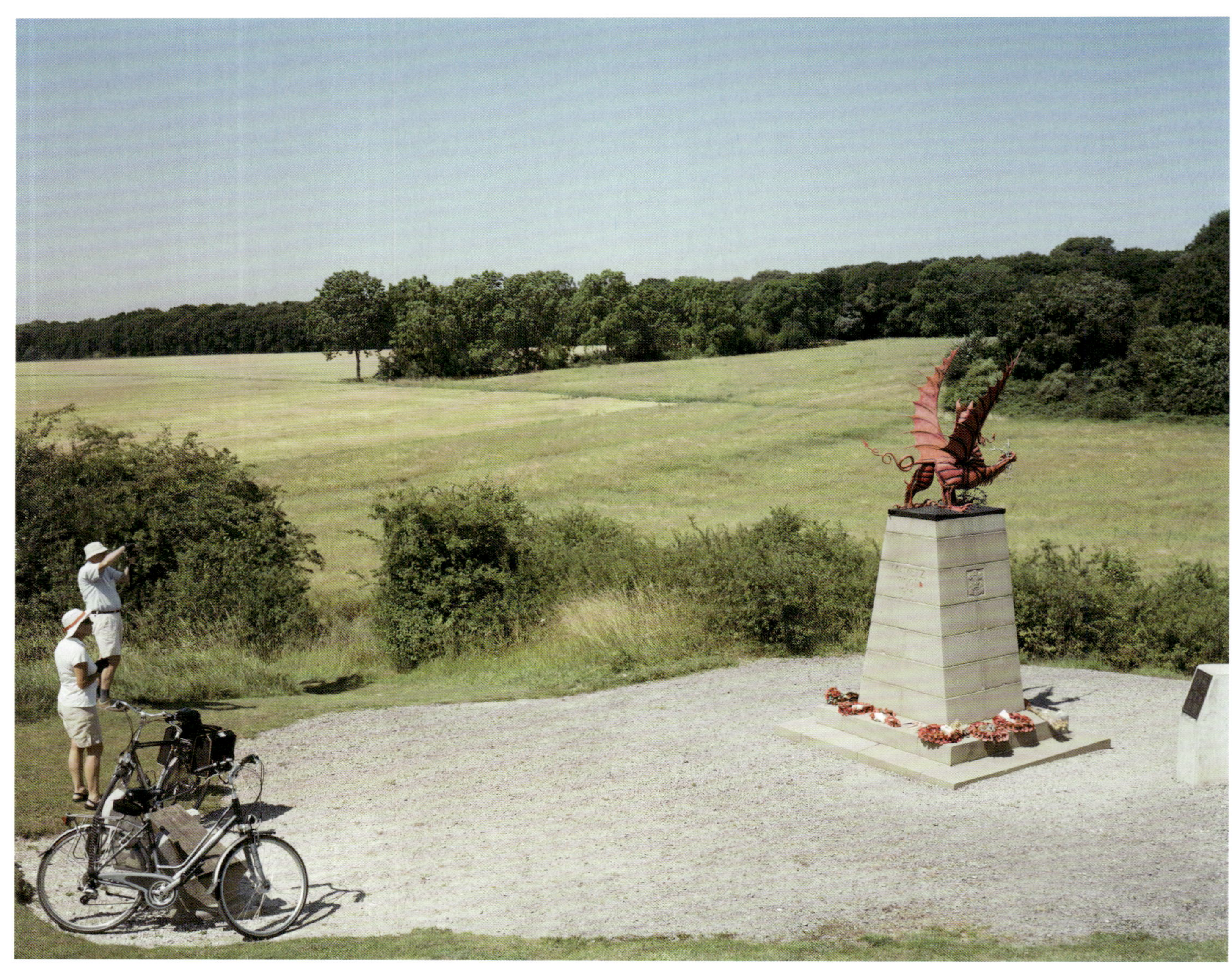

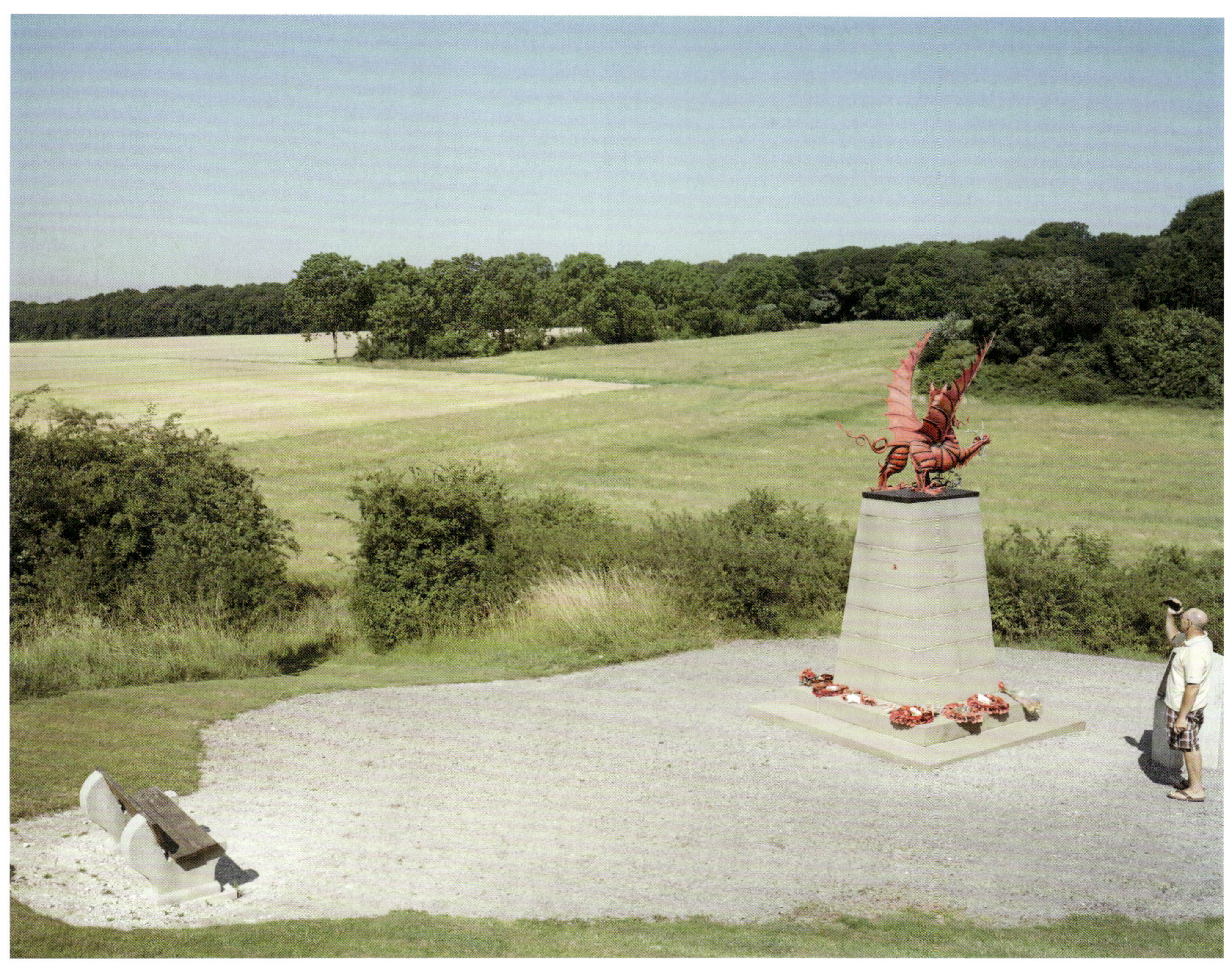

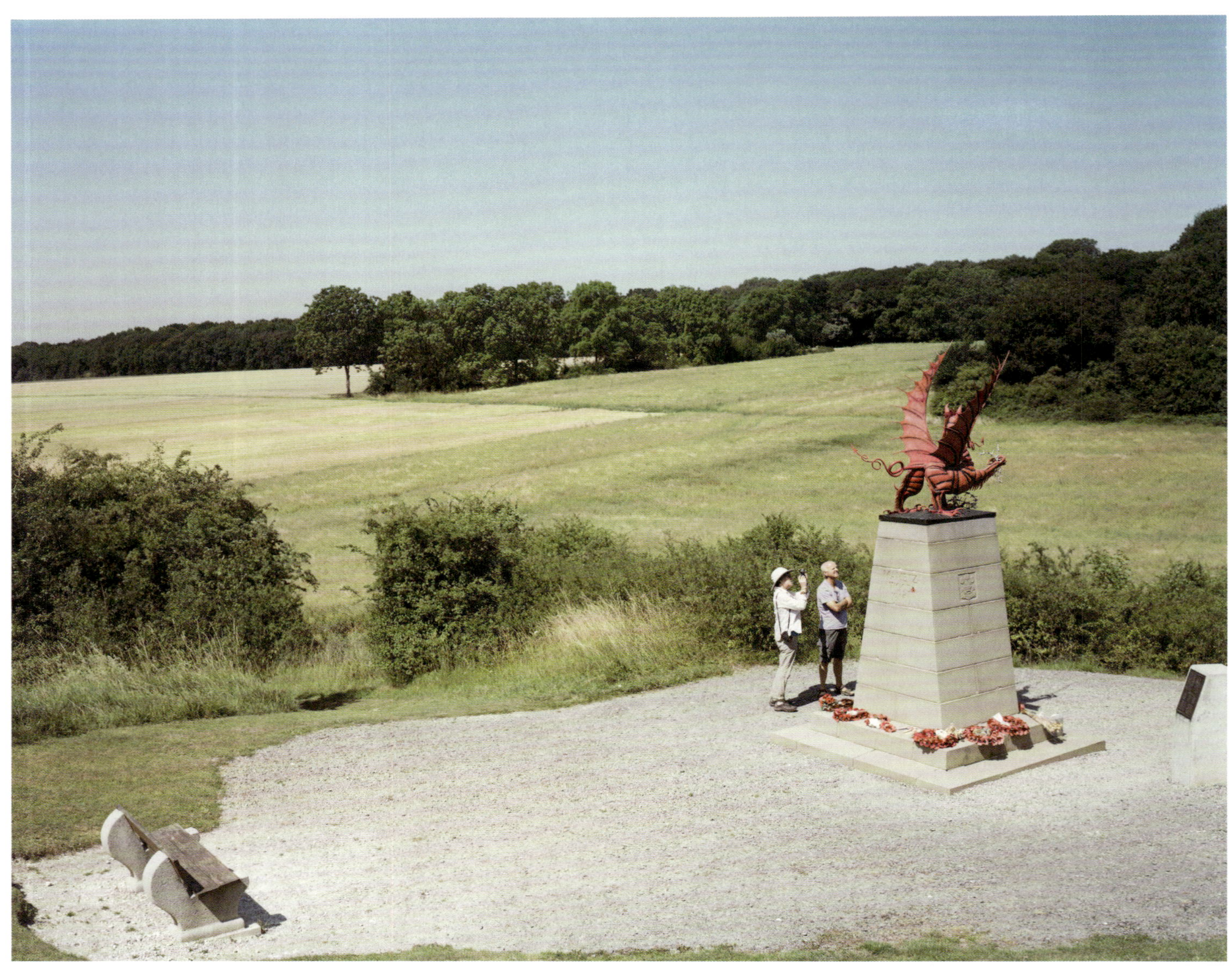

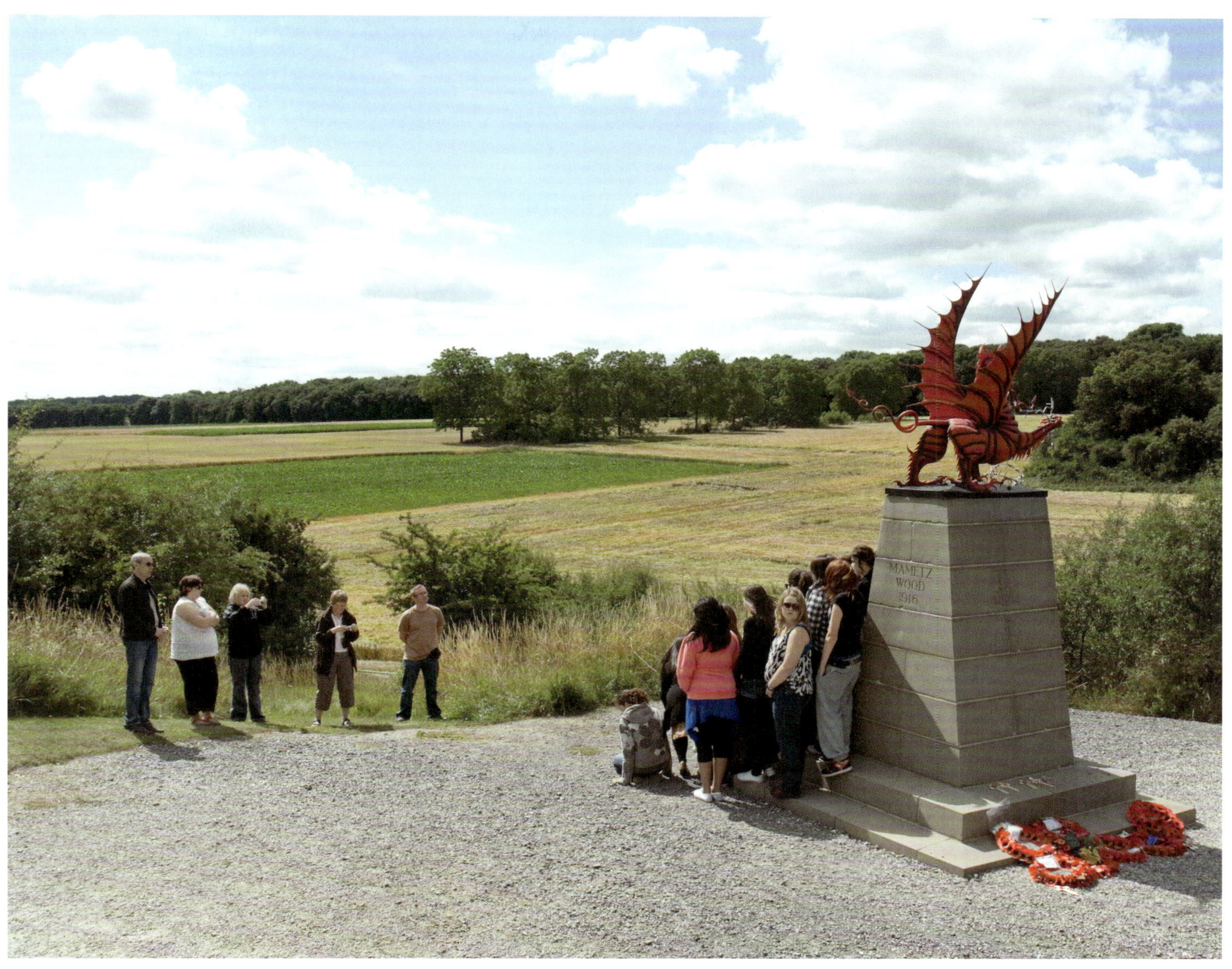

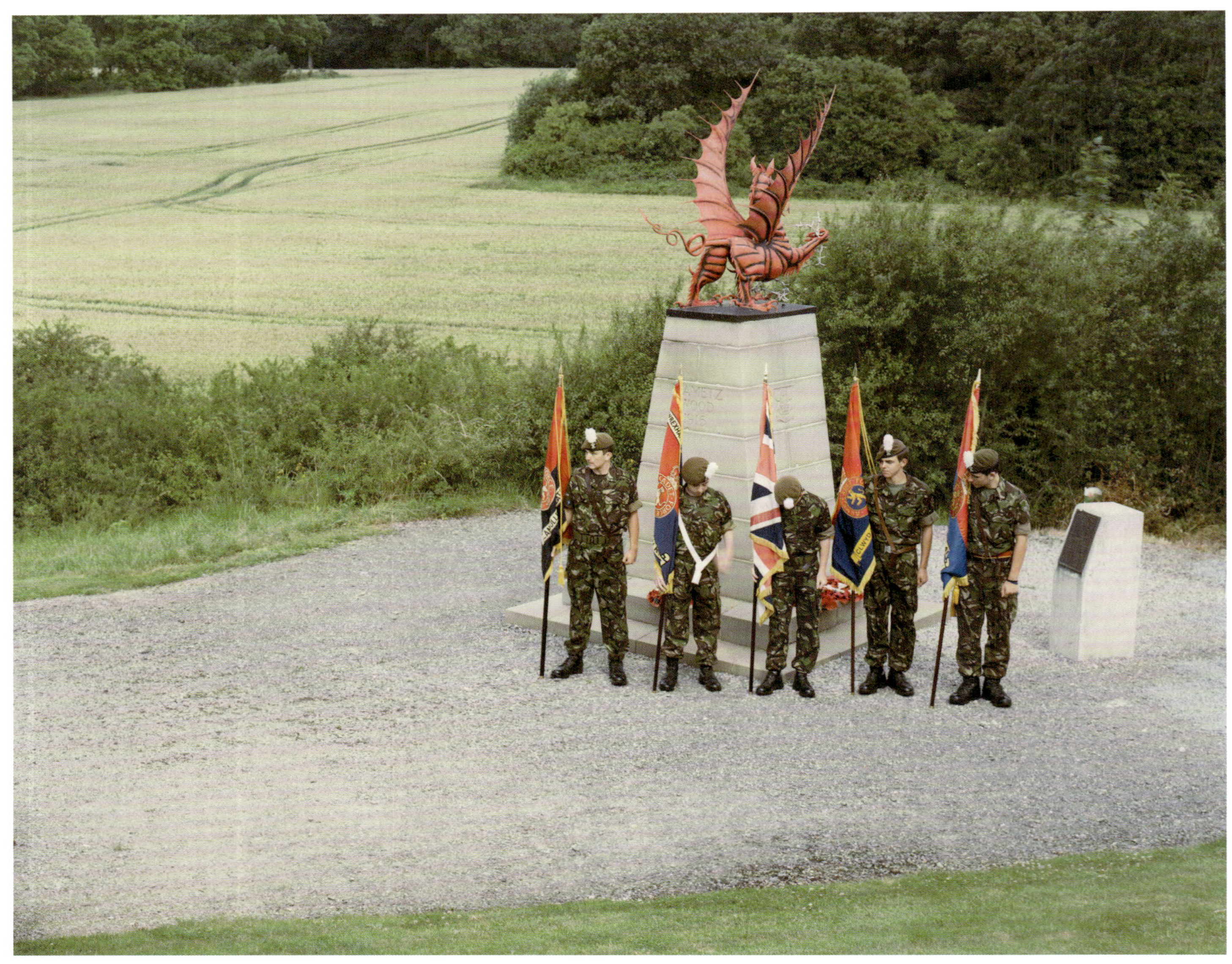

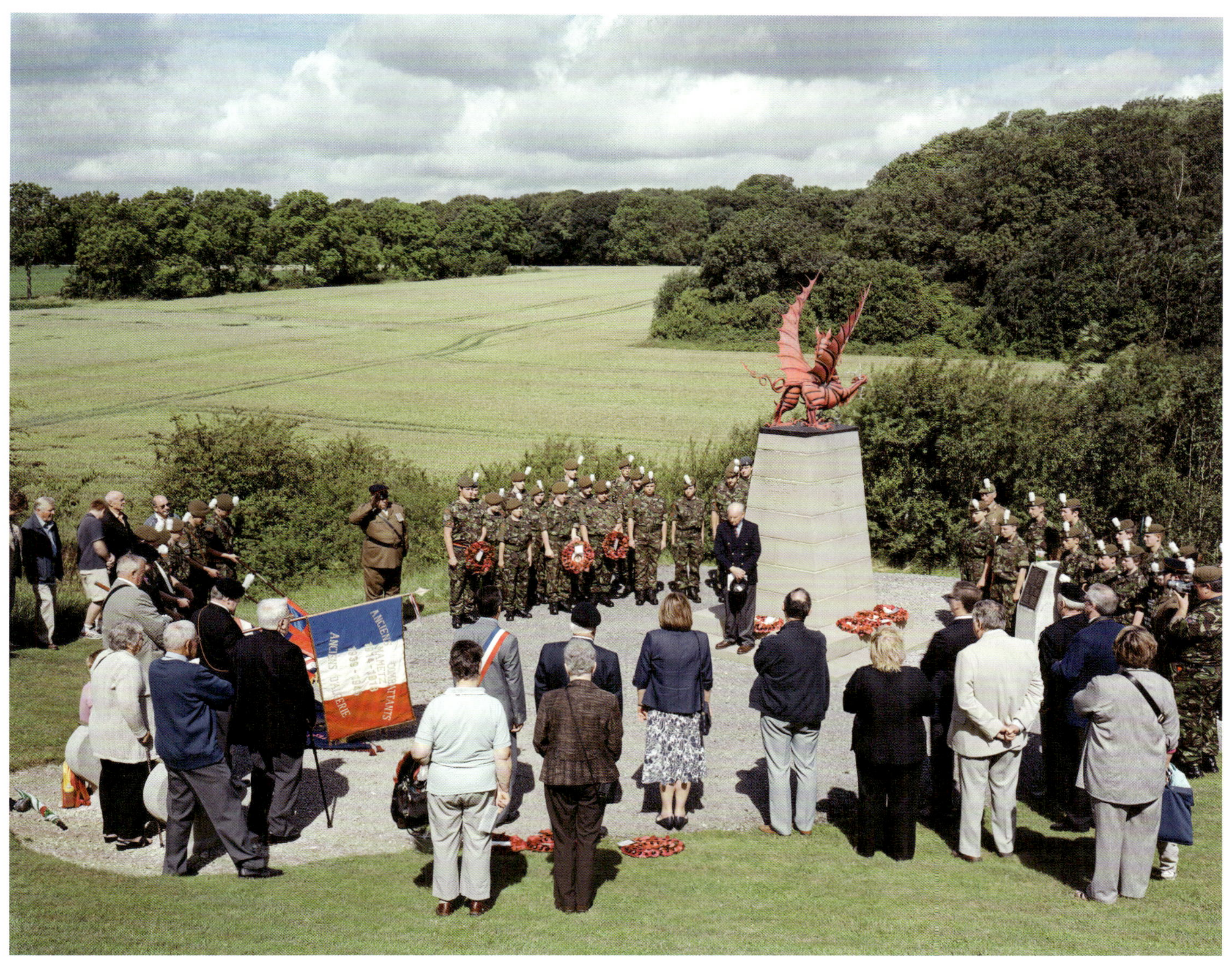

Mametz Wood:
The photographs of Aled Rhys Hughes

In Aled Rhys Hughes's photographs taken outside Mametz Wood rich sunlit corn fields end abruptly at a dark wall of trees. The juxtaposition of light and dark is an instance of the duality that characterises Hughes's photographic technique. Dark and light in this place are at once actual and metaphorical. Mametz Wood has a terrible history. Seen in relation to the open land the line starkly dividing light and dark calls up ideas of good and evil, past and present, life and death. In the shadowy interior of the wood dark and light are ambiguous, an entangled border more than a sharp division. In this liminal place, the evil of war was inextricably mixed with the heroism and endurance of men.

In the period 7-11 July 1916 Mametz Wood was the site of the 38th (Welsh) Division's first major engagement. Robin Barlow, in *Wales and World War One*, describes the wood that the Welsh troops were ordered to capture from the Germans:

> Mametz Wood occupied an area of approximately 220 acres, covered in thick undergrowth of hawthorn and briar intermingled with fallen trees and branches from previous bombardments, all of which would impede any progress on foot. Also on the floor of the Wood, there was a considerable amount of wire, which had been laid by the enemy during the respite from fighting after 1 July. There were still considerable numbers of standing trees of oak, beech and ash, averaging thirty to forty feet in height. The Wood measured about one mile from north to south and three-quarters of a mile from east to west at its widest point. Mametz Wood was divided by two straight rides and longitudinally by a third.

The thick wood occupied by elite German troops formed a formidable objective. This was made more lethal by the line of attack, which was down a slope and then uphill in open country. Thomas Dilworth, in *David Jones and the Great War*, draws on *In Parenthesis* and other first-hand accounts to describe the attack of 7 July:

> No man's land was 500 yards of wild, uncropped grass, thistles, wild flowers, and self-grown mustard and wheat. Like a mechanism perversely preset to move slowly, they walked across 60 yards of plateau, scurried down a steep 30 to 50 foot incline, and slowly walked up the bare, gradually rising slope towards high ground where the enemy waited, firing at them. The walk took four minutes, a passage through a maelstrom of rifle and machine-gun bullets, shrapnel and shell-casing fragments flying at every angle – a thousand potential deaths and maimings with no protecting cover. The noise was beyond hearing, the quaking earth erupting, the air thick with smoke, chalky dirt, steel, bits of flesh.

This was an episode, on a smaller scale, of the major Somme offensive, in which, on 1 July, the total number of British, French and German casualties was immense. Robin Barlow gives the figure of 911 NCOs and other ranks and thirty-seven officers belonging to the Welsh Division killed between 7-11 July in the battle of Mametz. 'In addition,' he says, 'many hundreds more men would have been posted missing, their bodies never recovered'. As Captain Llewlyn Wyn Griffith remarked, the bodies of the dead represented 'those who had to fall to prove to our command that machine guns can defend a bare slope'.

The next major advance on the wood on 10 July was more successful, and after ferocious fighting and in scenes of terrible confusion, the wood was partially taken. Under a German artillery bombardment, the Welsh Division began to withdraw on 11 July. The withdrawal was completed the following day, when the 21st Division, which cleared the remainder of the wood, relieved them. Some weeks later German troops recaptured Mametz Wood, which they held to the end of the war.

Was the battle of Mametz, in which so many young men on both sides were killed or wounded, a success for the Welsh? Assessments of both witnesses and historians differ. Siegfried Sassoon described the battle as 'a disastrous muddle with troops stampeding under machine-gun fire'. The historian, Colin Hughes, concluded that 'the Welsh Division, inexperienced and inadequately trained, pushed the cream of Germany's professional army back about one mile in most difficult conditions, an achievement that should rank with that of any division on the Somme'.

But how is success or failure to be assessed in such circumstances? Robin Barlow is right, surely, when he says: 'The name of Mametz Wood, perhaps like those of Aberfan or Senghenydd, is embedded deep in the Welsh psyche, immediately conjuring up images of needless loss of life, bravery, chaos and self-sacrifice'. But how can a photographer today, or any of us, know anything about the reality of the battle? As Llewelyn Wyn Griffith said: 'there were two kinds of men in the world – those who had been in the trenches, and the rest'.

This is a truth of which a sensitive visitor, such as Aled Rhys Hughes, is acutely aware. He will avoid voyeurism by acknowledging its risk. According to Robert Adams, the American photographer: 'What we hope for from the artist is help in discovering the significance of a place'. Hughes comes close to revealing the significance of Mametz Wood by acknowledging his distance from the events that made it famous. Moreover, he knows it as a place embedded in his psyche, as a Welshman. And he knows what the witnesses have told us, so that when he walks in Mametz Wood with his camera he will be mindful of a passage such as this from Llewelyn Wyn Griffith's *Up to Mametz*:

Years of neglect had turned the Wood into a formidable barrier, a mile deep. Heavy shelling of the Southern end had beaten down some of the young growth, but it had also thrown trees and large branches into a barricade. Equipment, ammunition, rolls of barbed wire, tins of food, gas-helmets and rifles were lying about everywhere. There were more corpses than men, but there were worse sights than corpses. Limbs and mutilated trunks, here and there a detached head, forming splashes of red against the green leaves, and, as in advertisement of the horror of our way of life and death, and of our crucifixion of youth, one tree held in its branches a leg, with its torn flesh hanging down over a spray of leaf.

Part 7 of David Jones's *In Parenthesis* covers the same ground as *Up to Mametz*. Jones was a Private in B Company, Griffith a Captain in C Company. They came through the battle, survived the war, and, some ten years after the war, wrote their remarkable accounts of the battle of Mametz Wood. *In Parenthesis*, one of the greatest of all war books, was what first drew Aled Rhys Hughes to Mametz Wood, which he has visited on several occasions, making photographic studies, and entering deeper into its mystery. The writings, and especially David Jones's epic poem, have influenced his sense of the place, whose meaning he explores in his photographs.

There is a significant connection between poetry and photography in relation to war. Since the advent of photography in the nineteenth century photographs have worked together with poetry in evoking war landscapes and revealing the reality of war. Photographs and poems have memorialised war and fixed its images in our minds. Thus, Roger Fenton's *Valley of the Shadow of Death* brings to the Crimean War battlefield associations with Tennyson's 'The Charge of the Light Brigade' and Psalm 23. We see the American Civil War battlefields through the photographs of Matthew Brady and his associates and through Walt Whitman's poems. If the former emphasize desolation, the latter express personal emotion – though this is not to say photographs lack emotion. Wilfred Owen collected photographs of the dead and maimed to show to ignorant civilians, and Owen's poems, together with photographs of the Western Front, have contributed to our understanding of the First World War.

Some modern thinkers, notably Susan Sontag and Roland Barthes, associate photographs with death. This is not only because they show dead people, as in gruesome pictures revealing the horror of war, but because they show what is past. Photography bears the mark of mortality, and is the art most confined by the past: it reminds us that once living subjects are dead; it isolates person or object or event, separating them from the stream of life. Actual photographs of the First World War picture landscapes of death, with dead or wounded men, ruined buildings, shattered trees, and torn earth. Some subliminal sense of these is likely to emerge into our consciousness from time to time as we look at Hughes's photographs, which contain signs of the carnage and devastation that once made a waste land of Mametz Wood. His subject, however, is by no means exclusively death or horror, any more than it is of *In Parenthesis*.

In Hughes's photographs the landscape in which Mametz Wood is situated appears today much as it would have done to the men of the 38th (Welsh) Division in July 1916. Except, of course, that we see it in the shadow of the slaughter that, for them, was to come. But the sun shines in these pictures of hilly chalk country interspersed with groups of trees, beyond the dark edge of Mametz Wood. To the troops arriving on 5 July 1916 with orders to take the wood, the landscape would have been reminiscent of parts of southern England, with which it shares geology and a history of cultivation. To them, it must have appeared at once homely and sinister. The names they gave to this French landscape, such as White Trench, Bunny Trench, Acid Drop Copse, and Caterpillar Wood, both designated military locations and laid claim to an uneasy intimacy. With hindsight, we know that the area that the men called Happy Valley, in which Jones's battalion went into reserve for brief respite on 8 July, became Death Valley. The sun still shines on it in Hughes's photograph of the area, but we see the innocent landscape with bitter knowledge.

Woods have been powerful presences in human history, and to this day they have kept something of their ancient aura. Woods are traditionally homely and alien, beautiful and sinister, 'dark' places in which the hero loses himself, and perhaps his life, or completes his quest. They are sacred in the dual sense of being both blessed and cursed, and they nourish a rich, ambivalent poetry. *In Parenthesis* includes an especially powerful evocation of the significance of woods. The scene occurs around Christmas 1915, some seven months before the attack on Mametz Wood, when John Ball, 'posted as 1st Day Sentry, sat on the fire-step; and looking upward, sees in a cunning glass the image of: his morning parapets, his breakfast-fire smoke, the twisted wood beyond':

> Across the very quiet of no-man's land came still some twittering. He found the wood, visually so near, yet for the feet forbidden by a great fixed gulf, a sight somehow to powerfully hold his mind. To the woods of all the world is this potency – to move the bowels of us.
>
> To groves always men come both to their joys and their undoing. Come lightfoot in heart's ease and school-free; walk on a leafy holiday with kindred and kind; come perplexedly with first loves – to tread the tangle frustrated, striking – bruising the green.

The evocation of Biez Copse as 'the woods of all the world' comprehends the whole range of human experience, with a wealth of allusions to Malory and Arthurian Romance, *Y Gododdin* and *The Golden Bough*, Celtic history and myth, and folksong. To woods men

Come with Merlin in his madness, for the pity of it; for the young men reaped like green barley,
for the folly of it.

The passage reinforces the intimacy between men and nature that characterizes *In Parenthesis*, and enhances the poignant imagery of men and trees entangled in a common destruction in Mametz Wood: 'stamen-twined and bruised pistilline/steel-shorn of style and ovary/leaf and blossoming/with flora-spangled khaki pelvises'. In Mametz Wood, the poetry of 'the woods of all the world', as perceived in Biez Copse, continues in a different key, and David Jones's depiction of the war shows graphically 'the pity of it', and 'the folly of it'.

The emotions of the scene recall Wilfred Owen and other poets, unsparing in their rendering of the pity and folly of the war. But with David Jones there is a difference. Begun ten years after the end of the war, *In Parenthesis* has the advantage of perspective. It combines the immediacy of terrible experience with a vision of ultimate meaning in the form of religious myth. Through images such as that of 'the young men reaped like green barley' David Jones intimates a metaphysical order, which is sacrificial and redemptive. It is a Christian vision that assimilates ancient pagan myth.

Aled Rhys Hughes's view of Mametz Wood has certain affinities with this vision of a restorative metaphysical order. He is not, however, a trespasser on the ground of the men who fought there, men like David Jones and Llewelyn Wyn Griffith, who won the right of a larger understanding. Questioning marks the spirit in which Hughes approaches Mametz Wood. Robert Adams, in *Beauty in Photography*, a book with special significance for Hughes, describes Beauty as 'a synonym for the coherence and structure underlying life'. Art affirms Form: 'a framework that is larger than we are, encompassing totality invulnerable to our worst behaviour and most corrosive anxieties'. These words can be applied, with caution, to what Hughes shows in his pictures of Mametz Wood.

Seen in the light of 'a framework that is larger than we are', the beauty of Hughes's photographs shows in Mametz Wood and the surrounding land a restored nature and agriculture – a life continuous with the life that preceded the war. But things do not go on the same, blotting out memory. The landscape shows stark contrasts of light and dark, and the interior of the wood is green, with natural shadows that also evoke the darkening of hindsight. Light against dark suggests conflicting opposites: life and death, good and evil, peace and war. Shadows represent memories, but also foreground indefiniteness, the difficulty of seeing clearly, of knowing exactly what we are looking at. The uncertainty is first in the mind of the photographer. He shares his questions with us. What does it mean, this landscape of memory – other men's memory – this landscape of the dead, with shell craters and trench systems that look like ancient earthworks, and physical mementoes of the war lying among leaves and fallen timber?

A picture of branches fallen crosswise may suggest Llewlyn Wyn Griffith's 'crucifixion of youth'. But, as Hughes knows, it is not for a visitor long after the battle to impose a meaning on the place. Meanings may, however, be suggested. The fact of the many young lives lost or ruined, together with the witness of writers who participated in the battle, haunt the photographer, and help to determine what he sees. However much he observes the delicate beauty of new growth, the pressure of appalling memory makes his seeing ambivalent. Duality is written into the landscape and the photographer emphasises it through use of scale and compositional rhythms – in sunlit, open cornland and dark wall of the wood, in chalky, flinty fields pitted by craters and harrowed by trenches, in shadow and light among the trees. Some analogies with painting suggest themselves. In Paul Nash's post-war paintings of southern England, for example, the landscapes remember his war paintings. The 'new world' men have made, the world of dead men and shattered trees in cratered landscapes, has become assimilated to the ancient burial sites, and to the very configuration of the rolling chalkland hills.

The risk of voyeurism is a challenge to the photographer, as to any visitor or viewer. The Mametz War Memorial, sculpted by David Petersen and erected in 1987, makes a bold statement. The Welsh Red Dragon tearing at the barbed wire in which it is entangled says what it means. Hughes's photograph of young soldiers of today paying formal respect at the memorial make a poignant image, reminding us how young many of the dead were, and warning us of the fate that may await these young men. But what are the motives of tourists with cameras? Do they remember the bitter humour with which the fighting men ironically foresaw 'a Cook's tourist to the Devastated Areas'? Hughes certainly remembers; he knows that by 1919 Michelin's illustrated guidebook to the Somme had appeared, and Mametz village was being talked about as a picturesque ruin. He takes his pictures in full knowledge of the irony. His emotions are complex, and guilt is part of them. This, though, is not disabling. It is, rather, a moral quality, and a creative unease, which determines him to meet what Rowan Williams calls the photographer's challenge to 'stereotyped images and stock of sentimental response'.

As in his photographs of the Welsh landscape and coast, Aled Rhys Hughes is an artist drawn to liminal and numinous places, places where a patient artist attentive to mysterious presences may discern a sense of metaphysical order. Open to meanings not of his own making, he has a keen sense of what may be intuited but cannot be easily seen or shown. For the soldiers themselves, the battlegrounds, where they lived with death, were haunted places. The Western Front generated in the men a sense of the uncanny, as memoirs and art of the war show. *In Parenthesis*, more than any other book, captures this atmosphere of mystery, in a place charged with the presence of death. In this respect,

its distinguishing feature is David Jones's use of pagan Celtic myth and Arthurian wasteland imagery. As a Welshman, Hughes is especially sensitive to the way in which this illuminates the life and death struggle enacted in Mametz Wood.

Woods are both naturally and symbolically mysterious places. Even today, any wood contains an echo of the primeval wildwood, and of forests that for centuries were dangerous places, the abode of robbers and outlaws, the lair of wild animals. For Britons, and especially for the Welsh, their aura recalls holy groves, places of worship and sacrifice for their Celtic ancestors. Any wood is both inviting and daunting, making us pause at the threshold with a sense of fearful excitement. What will we find if we walk or push our way in? Will we become lost? What is true of any wood is immeasurably truer of Mametz Wood. As Hughes's photographs show, it is naturally alive with green, leafy trees and undergrowth; but it is also a dark place, a place of evil memory, where the photographer walks with uncertainty. One of his most evocative photographs shows the shadow of the Welsh Dragon Memorial. The shadow lying on land outside the wood points along the line of advance to the dark wall of trees. What remains of all that heroic sacrifice but shadows?

As well as shadow, Mametz Wood is full of mementoes. Sometimes, like the branches fallen crosswise, these form natural symbols. More often, they are enigmatic – signs that raise questions. Some we can only see in the photographs by looking closely – as the photographer has looked, requiring of the viewer an equivalent attentiveness. A faded photograph pinned to a tree suggests a story we can only guess at. Does it show a soldier killed or wounded in battle, and placed in the wood by a descendant as an act of homage? The wood is full of fragments telling unknown stories. We know what poppies mean. But what is the meaning of the numerous small Welsh flags attached to trees? Do they lay claim to the place for Wales? And what would that tell us about Welsh nationality and its debt to historical memory? The name Mametz may resonate in the mind with Aberfan and Senghenydd. As a grievous event, it may be embedded in the Welsh psyche alongside Gruffudd ab yr Ynad Coch's poem on the death of Llyweln ap Gruffudd, when 'the oaks beat together'.

Entering Mametz Wood through Hughes's photographs we are entering this psyche. This is a place of old wounds, mental wounds, as real as the remains of trench systems, and of pride at heroic sacrifice. We may think of the sculpture of 'The Dying Gaul', the noble figure in which David Jones saw the Celtic 'defeat tradition'. The tradition is profoundly ambivalent, for upon the memory of defeat the Welsh have founded their survival as a nation. This is what can be seen in the spirit of Mametz Wood as Hughes reveals it: in half-light and darkness, in signs of the past in the present, in images of life and death. It can be seen too in contrasts between sharp definition and blurred focus, which emphasises uncertainty.

Mametz Wood was where men and nature underwent a mutually destructive action. Here, natural growth was subjected to mechanical destruction, and men and their machines were entangled in undergrowth and killed by falling trees. Human and natural powers were locked in deadly embrace, as were the Welsh and German soldiers. *In Parenthesis* is founded upon this polarity, as we see at the conclusion to the passage evoking 'the woods of all the world':

> Keep date with the genius of the place – come with a weapon or effectual branch – and here this winter copse might well be special to Diana's Jack, for none might attempt it, but by perilous bough-plucking.
>
> Draughtsman at Army made note on a blue-print of the significance of that grove as one of his strong-points; this wooded rise as the gate of their enemies, a door at whose splintered posts, Janus-wise emplacements shield an automatic fire.

In his later work, David Jones would develop the two kinds of 'significance' shown here – poetic, mythological, religious in opposition to the mechanically functional – into his philosophy of conflict between sacred sign and utility. Aled Rhys Hughes, too, is an artist who evokes 'the genius of the place'; and in his photographs of Mametz Wood he shows how the war brought men and nature together to share an intimacy that destroyed both.

The war created a literal closeness to the earth. They dug into it, seeking shelter; they were drowned in waterlogged trenches and craters; they were entangled in branches and crushed by falling trees. It created, too, a sense of kinship between men and nature, a common suffering, seen in a kind of equivalence between broken men and shattered trees. This intimate relationship between suffering men and ravaged nature appears in writings and paintings and contemporary photographs. What can be said of it positively is that it has influenced the modern ecological imagination.

It is with this imagination, in knowledge of the close relationship between men and nature, that Hughes approaches Mametz Wood. He shows a tree severed from its roots, hanging, without ground to grow in – an actual tree, but also a tree that bears the larger, symbolic significance. The image both reminds us of what the war did to men and trees, and prevents easy thoughts about nature's regenerative power. But that power is not denied: Mametz Wood today is once more a living wood. Another photograph shows a live shell among corn, which the farmer has ploughed round, as the agricultural year continues in spite of the war, and the earth absorbs its mementoes. Artillery shells rest by the base of a tree, unnatural but harmless occupants of the wood. Wood has grown round a shell, in what looks like a protective embrace. Other photographs show gnarls on trees caused by shells or bullets, but not unlike natural growths. Some look like totems. Overgrown trench systems might be ancient tumuli. A shell that looks like a strange creature has taken up residence on the woodland floor. Mametz Wood, originally used for hunting, has its own wild life, which includes deer and wild boar. Since the war, shell cases and other military fragments have become native to the place.

The photographs show how the fallen are remembered throughout the wood. Crosses and wreaths of poppies make small, but definite, statements of human value against the magnitude of the trees. They are not leaves, but they look as if they belong here. Welsh flags maintain a strong Welsh presence. They are commemorative, but we may wonder what claim they are also making, since flags are used to lay claim to places. This wood in France is a Welsh wood, a wood of Welsh memory, an outpost of the Welsh nation. But do the flags also claim victory? Here, we return to our question on first entering the wood: what is victory in such circumstances? It is what the photographs show that makes us especially cautious about offering opinions or making judgements.

Hughes is careful not to interfere with mementoes he comes upon in the wood. He has, however, photographed examples of trench art, such as a candleholder made from a shell case, and a paper knife made from a bullet. Each object speaks of a story we do not know. Objects represent the German dead too: a lamp, the sole of a boot, a belt buckle. Most evocatively, the photograph of a photograph: a funeral card that prays for 20-year-old Leonhard Schachtner, Soldat, 'Tod fürs Vaterland'. One name, one brief history, but it stands for the tragedy of all the young lives lost in the battle of Mametz Wood.

Symbols occur as if naturally through the photographer's art. Cornland and ploughed, chalky fields, rolling hills, the dark wall of the wood, all reveal the presence of the past they have absorbed, a tragic modern history assimilated to the ancient dead. In the photographs we are seeing a landscape almost a century after a battle. At the same time, we are seeing it much as the men of the 38th (Welsh) Division saw it on 5 July 1916, with the homely yet alien hills at their backs, and the formidable wood, concealing the enemy, below and in front of them. Taken outside the wood, a photograph shows docks, like blood, moving towards the dark wall.

The men knew Mametz Wood as the Queen of the Woods on the Somme battlefield. David Jones gave the name a special significance in *In Parenthesis*:

> The Queen of the Woods has cut bright bows of various flowering.
>
> These knew her influential eyes. Her awarding hands can pluck for each their fragile prize.
>
> She speaks to them according to precedence. She knows what's due to this elect society. She can choose twelve gentlemen. She knows who is most lord between the high trees and on the open down.

Colin Hughes concludes his study, *David Jones: The man who was on the field*, by recalling Jones's reaction to being shown photographs of Mametz Wood fifty years after the battle:

> 'It is clear from the photographs' wrote David Jones in 1969, remembering the wood only as a shell-torn waste-land, 'that the Queen of the Woods has revivified her groves. It reminds me,' he added, 'of the line from the folk song John Barleycorn,
>
> "And Barleycorn stood up again and that surprised them all."

The folk song speaks of regeneration, death that gives rise to new life. It was poetry, in the form of religious myth, which for Jones ultimately held the significance of the battle of Mametz Wood. This was grounded in love, love of dead comrades, but also the sacrificial love that he perceived as the meaning of the universe. Llewelyn Wyn Griffith also saw the war in terms of his Christian inheritance. But his judgement of the battle was more sombre than Jones's:

> Added to the burden of fatigue and grief, we were governed
> by a dark feeling of personal failure. Mametz Wood was taken,
> but not by us, it seemed; we were the rejected of Destiny, men
> whose services were not required. The dead were the chosen,
> and Fate had forgotten us in its eager clutching at the men
> who fell; they were the richer prize. They captured Mametz
> Wood, and in it they lie.

Jorge Luis Borges, in his lecture 'The Divine Comedy', quotes Homer, 'the gods weave misfortunes for men, so that the generations to come will have something to sing about', and Mallarmé, "'tout aboutit en un livre', everything ends up in a book". Borges concludes: 'something remains, and that something is history or poetry, which are not essentially different'. This chimes with Griffith's discovery:

> Common clay as we were, and far enough removed as we
> thought ourselves from the spun glass of the poet's imagining,
> we found ourselves betrayed into the very emotions they had
> sung. That the prose of war should prove the truth of poetry's
> tale of man's feeling – that it should now be easy to believe
> that some of those magic lines were indeed a reflection of the
> real thoughts of real men and women – that was an astonish-
> ing discovery.

It is true that what we know of the battle of Mametz Wood is poetry. This may be interpreted, in the broad sense of the word, as vision: the vision of *In Parenthesis*, and of *Up to Mametz*. Aled Rhys Hughes sees with his own eyes as an artist, but he also draws upon what these books have shown him. The result is a sequence of photographs that have their own visionary quality. In achieving this, Hughes's art helps us to discover the significance of the place.

– JEREMY HOOKER

Acknowledgements

The images in this publication would not have been possible without the financial support from The Arts Council of Wales, for which I am very grateful. Not only has Jeremy Hooker written a most insightful essay for the book, our conversations and correspondences about 'ground' have been catalysts for ideas and many of my images. The staff at The National Library of Wales have opened their David Jones collection for me to explore, and use his map of Mametz as part of this publication. I'm also grateful to Phil Davies, Secretary of the South Wales Branch of the Western Front Association, Martine Warlop with who I walked through the wood in search of 'witness trees', and to Andy Satherley-Bell, Peter Finnemore, Nigel Williams, Paul Cabuts and Shaun McDermott for their assistance and reviews of the work. The support and encouragement from my family throughout the past seven years has been absolute, and I thank them for it.

Photographic Notes

The Photographs were all made with a large format film camera, the most cumbersome piece of apparatus I could take to the wood, the visual quality however, and the slowness of the image making process was at one with my pensive approach.

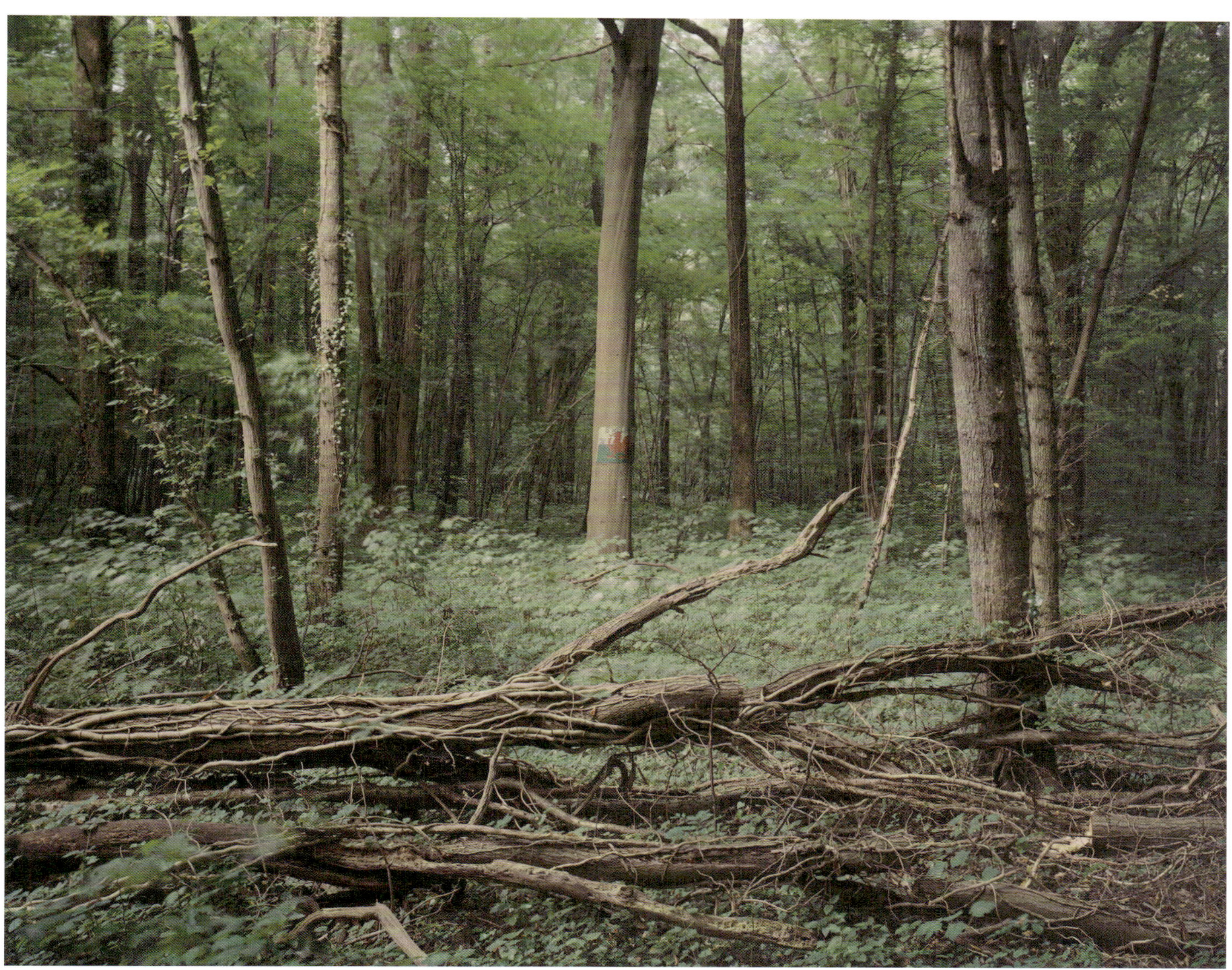